# A Physician Under
# the Nazis

## Memoirs of Henry Glenwick

Edited by
David Glenwick

Foreword by Thane Rosenbaum

**Hamilton Books**
A member of
The Rowman & Littlefield Publishing Group
*Lanham • Boulder • New York • Toronto • Plymouth, UK*

**Copyright © 2011 by**
**Hamilton Books**
4501 Forbes Boulevard
Suite 200
Lanham, Maryland 20706
Hamilton Books Acquisitions Department (301) 459-3366

Estover Road
Plymouth PL6 7PY
United Kingdom

Library of Congress Control Number: 2010931126
ISBN: 978-0-7618-5136-3 (paperback : alk. paper)
eISBN: 978-0-7618-5137-0

To the memory of Alexander Sholom Gliniewiecki (1938-1942),
who didn't have a chance

—D.G.

# Contents

# Foreword

The memoirs of those who survived the Holocaust have, over the years, grown to produce a critical mass of reflections on mass murder. Now we have the contribution of Henry Glenwick, in a wonderful book edited by his son, David.

Leo Tolstoy wrote: "Happy families are all alike; every unhappy family is unhappy in its own way." So much for families, but what of those for whom happiness and unhappiness are no longer descriptively relevant, where the range of emotion swings far more radically in one direction on the dial meter of sorrow, where there are descending states of melancholy and no ladders of recovery? Sadness is not quite sad enough and yet lasts an eternity; black is no longer the darkest shade on the palette of the human psyche.

Happiness and whatever is its opposite apply to ordinary events and the people who live them. These measurements have little meaning in the world of atrocity.

Hundreds of thousand of Holocaust survivors each witnessed barbarism and inhumanity on a grand scale. If unhappiness is a guarantee to its own equivalent uniqueness, then what does an intimate familiarity with madness ensure? What Holocaust survivors saw was unspeakable, and yet many chose to write down their memories, trying to capture in words and sentences observations and feelings that have no true human vocabulary.

Why would anyone wish to relive that level of trauma, to force the mind to give voice and shape and image to the monstrous and grotesque? Part of the improbable miracle of survival—the returning to the world of the living—is that it required a severe compromising of self-awareness: In order to start over, the past must become archived in a warehouse of memory that permits little or no private access. There is a forbidden line of demarcation on the conscience and consciousness. It's not the same as forgetting. It is simply memory in relief, the eclipse of any useful recollection.

What we have learned from survivors is that this survival technique lasted only so long. The ability to hold off the memories eventually faded. And what returned was a furious form of remembrance.

The result brought thousands of oral history projects and hundreds of memoirs. Together they stand not only as deeply affecting tributes to human loss and grief but also as monuments of human fortitude and resilience. They are acts of witness and testimony, a transcription—both oral and written—that has the transcendent aim to both remember the dead and remind the future of what is inhumanly possible.

Primo Levi wrote: "No words can be used to describe this offense, the demolition of a man." One of the world's greatest memoirists acknowledged his own limitations when it came to recording the indescribable. And yet he tried and produced a masterpiece.

Like Primo Levi, who was an Italian chemist, Henry Glenwick was first a scientist and physician before he became a victim of the Holocaust. The clinical mind of a man trained to recognize and relieve sickness makes for an acutely observant, if not emotionally detached, chronicler of pathologies too vast and unfathomable for Petri dishes and microscopes. And yet, in a calmly reflective voice, almost standing outside of himself, Henry Glenwick has told the world his story. Somewhere within these pages rests the diagnosis of a man who traveled back and forth and yet, in the end, was determined to take one final look.

Thane Rosenbaum

# Acknowledgments

A number of persons have contributed meaningfully to the publication of these memoirs and merit my deepest appreciation. To all of you, I am extremely grateful: Pavel Ilyin and Lucy Meyerovich of the United States Holocaust Memorial Museum, for the invaluable map; Thomas Heffernan of Robert Cook Associates and Jean Nudd of the United States National Archives, for the illuminating genealogy; Thane Rosenbaum, for his insightful and reflective foreword; Tracy Prout, Anne Leicht, Maria Barbieri, and Margaux Bruzzese for their responsive and unfailingly good-humored typing assistance; Samantha Kirk, my editor at Hamilton Books, for her wise guidance and combination of gentle prompting and flexibility; and Susan Cane, for her unflagging support and perceptive suggestions. My thanks for helping to make this a much richer work than it otherwise would have been.

Finally, my son, Michael, and my mother, Celia, deserve especial, heartfelt mention, both for their encouragement of this effort and for being—by his embracing of possibility and her indefatigability of spirit—constant sources of inspiration to me.

David Glenwick

# Editor's Introduction

*A Physician Under the Nazis* had its genesis as oral history, being the product of a series of interviews that I, then a graduate student in psychology, conducted with my father in the early 1970s. Following the transcription of the interview tapes, my father supplemented the material with further detail and observations, and I provided additional editing for readability. In the years since then, the manuscript has circulated among relatives and friends, helping to illuminate one family's history within the context of the Holocaust.

Rereading these memoirs more than three decades later, with an awareness of the survivor generation's imminent passing from the scene (my father having died in 1995), I believe that they possess interest and value beyond their original intended audience. It has been noted that all Holocaust survivors' stories are, in a sense, the same but that each is unique in its own telling. In the present work may be found the combination of luck, acts of kindness (by both Jews and non-Jews), and resourcefulness that is common to most survivor accounts. At the same time, its depiction of a Jewish physician who served in succession both the Russian Communists and the Nazis provides a distinctive window on the Holocaust experience.

One of my ongoing research interests as a clinical psychologist has been the effects of stress on behavior, as well as the ways in which people attempt to cope with, and moderate the impact of, stressors and trauma. This research, carried out within a traditional scientific framework, has been primarily quantitative in nature. Narratives, such as the present volume, serve as a complement to such data-based approaches. By offering first-person perspectives on facing adversity, they provide an alternative, but equally valid, way of knowing.

In editing the manuscript for publication, my aim has been to increase its accessibility to a general readership without altering its content, voice, and meaning. I hope that readers will indeed find meaning in the personal history and reflections contained in the following pages.

# Chapter One

# A Childhood in Warsaw

I was born in Warsaw, Poland (which, at that time, was under Russian occupation), on May 25, 1909, to Samuel and Judith Gliniewiecki. An only child, I was born in the apartment of my maternal grandparents (the Schulweises), who lived at 44 Dzika Street. After World War I the name of this street was changed to Zamenhof Street to honor Dr. Ludovic Zamenhof, the creator of the international Esperanto language, who had lived on it.

I remember a few stories told about my early childhood. When I was three years old, my first picture was taken, in which I sat holding a big hoop. When I returned home, I told my maternal grandfather in Yiddish: "Ich hob mich schon gelost," which means "I let them already take my picture." I started my very early years in a Jewish cheder (pronounced "Khey'-der"), a kind of parochial elementary school. There, at the age of five, I was taught how to read Hebrew and began learning "chumash," the Pentateuch (the first five books of the Hebrew Bible). A couple of years later I also started to have teachers in secular subjects at home after cheder. My father made sure that I never had any free time to play. During the entire daytime I was in cheder, and in the evening I had my extra teacher, which most of the other Jewish children did not have.

When I was about ten I went with my family to a summer resort, Ciechocinek. There is a photo of me there standing and holding a stick made from a branch of a tree. I recall that while we were in Ciechocinek we ran into Dr. Centnerschwer, the doctor who had taken care of my mother after I was born. My mother had had quite a bit of trouble after my delivery; due to a blood clot and inflammation in a leg she was in bed for about three months, and for the rest of her life she had a permanent red discoloration of the part of the leg where this phlebitis had been.

When I was a young child, my father was working for other people in textiles as a sales clerk in wholesale and retail firms. Later, he had his own business, very frequently with partners. He was an expert in appraising the quality of merchandise and an excellent salesman. However, he found it difficult to get to the business on time in the morning. My mother and I were early risers, but my father always liked to sleep about a half hour longer and we had to wake him up. Sometimes he would plead with us, "Please let me sleep another few minutes." And then he was not very quick, taking his time washing and dressing, then putting on his tallis (prayer shawl) and tefillin (phylacteries) and praying. About every two weeks he would go to Lodz, which was known as the "Polish Manchester," where the textile industry was centered and where most wholesalers from Warsaw bought their merchandise. Usually he left in the morning by train, but it would not be unusual for him to miss his first train. Because there were frequent trains he would say that he never missed a train: "If I do not go with the one, I will go with the next." I also remember that whenever we had to go to a wedding or some other family affair, my mother was not the one who was late. The two of us were always ready, my father was never ready, and we were always standing and standing, while he was taking his sweet time getting ready. He was always very well dressed and groomed, his trousers perfectly pressed and his clothing and tie impeccable.

It is worth mentioning that, even in Warsaw, average apartments at this time did not have any showers or bathtubs. There were toilets and only cold running water, no warm running water. In order to take a bath one had to heat water for the bathtub, or, in the absence of a bathtub in the apartment, one had to go to public or private baths. We used to go to private baths, which were not cheap nor close to the house. In the kitchens, there were gas burners, which were used for daily cooking, but there were also stoves using coal and wood, where major cooking or baking was done. The houses, except for some new ones in the very expensive neighborhoods of Warsaw, had no central heating. There were different types of furnaces in the apartments, usually high, nearly up to the ceiling, and covered with nice large tiles. In the winter, a fire had to be made with coal and wood every day in the furnace. The heated tiles kept the rooms warm until the next day. Usually one or two adjoining rooms shared a furnace. Most people had bins for coal storage in the basement of the building. Some people had bins built in the apartment (in the kitchen), where they kept a supply of coal and wood.

Let me return to the subject of my father's occupation. He spent most of his day at his business, not coming home for lunch, which we called "second breakfast." People usually ate dinner, which was the big meal, at about three or four o'clock in the afternoon. This was during business hours, so my father was busy and often unable to come home on time. If he had a client with a big wholesale order, he would spend a few hours making up the order for him. If he started with the order at one o'clock or two o'clock and became involved for three or more hours, he would come home at five or six o'clock to heat his three o'clock dinner, having a headache by that time. Then he would go back to the business and would come home at eight or nine in the evening, when we all had a little dairy bite referred to as "supper."

My father had his business in the textile section of Warsaw, which was concentrated on one street, Gesia Street, a short block of about twenty buildings, which was also the textile center for the larger surrounding area of many towns quite far from Warsaw. These were high-rise buildings, about four or five stories high, with most of the apartments and stores occupied by textile businesses. In the vicinity were other business centers; the next block was a famous street with silk and lace, and another was the center of the leather business for a large part of Poland. Merchants from small towns would come here to buy their goods. My father's clients were from various towns and would come every few weeks to buy merchandise for their stores. When they sold out their goods, they would come back. Most of his business was on open credit and promissory notes. These merchants were usually not very wealthy, and every few years some of them customarily would go bankrupt. Usually my father would settle with them, writing off part of the debt, and then continue doing business with them again. There were some business people in these small towns who were rich, whose credit was good, and who never would default, but they were few. Everybody would run after them when they came to Warsaw to obtain their merchandise.

As I mentioned before, my father often had partners. Some of them gave him trouble, and after a few years they would break up the partnership, with resulting losses. Despite this, he always managed to make a comfortable living, buying everything of the best quality and usually being generous. In the summer we would go to the country, renting a place for a month or two, mostly my mother and myself, with my father coming out for weekends. He was often late, catching the last train to get out Friday to come before candle-lighting time. My father liked things to be just the way he wanted them, becoming irritated and temperamental if he did not find them that way. Many times I felt sorry for my mother, who was the calmer and quieter type, trying to please her dear husband. She was a good-natured person and was liked very much, not only by close relatives but also by many distant relatives and neighbors. When I came to this country in 1946, my uncles, Irving and Maurice Schulweis, spoke about her, their sister, with love and deep affection. She was the older daughter; there were two daughters and five sons in the family. The next-to-oldest child, she was like a mother to her brothers, as my grandmother was a rather selfish person and relied a lot on my mother for the care of the family.

My father got along quite well with most of my mother's brothers. I recall with affection one of them, my uncle Jacob, who was a very fine and intelligent person. He was once in a business partnership with my father, and they remained forever very close. Jumping ahead for a moment, I recall meeting him in the Warsaw ghetto in 1942, when he told me with a broken heart that the Nazis had taken away both of his sons. He never saw them again. A year later he, as well as all of the other Jews in the ghetto, were taken away, and he perished. Another of my mother's brothers, Mayer, also was once in partnership with my father, but this partnership did not last long and did not end too happily. Once the partnership broke up they never spoke to each other again. Although the fathers never made up, the families made up later, and I would go to Mayer's home, where I met my first girlfriend, a friend of Judith, my uncle Mayer's daughter. Judith's older brother David left home for Israel (then Palestine) at the age of sixteen or seventeen as a "halutz" (pioneer) and never returned to Poland.

My mother had one sister, younger than herself, Cesia. She lived in a small town near Warsaw where her husband had a business. They had two daughters. When the Germans occupied Poland during World War II and chased out all the Jews from the small towns, Cesia's family lost everything and came to Warsaw. Later they were exterminated.

I was not as involved with my father's family, although I was close with some of them. After my Bar Mitzvah I went for a summer vacation to Ostrowiec, where my father had a sister, Esther Sherman, and where my father's oldest brother, Isaac, also was living. Because these two families were in different kinds of businesses, one had dinner at two o'clock in the afternoon and the other at seven or eight o'clock in the evening. Between the two of them I had to eat two dinners each day—I had a very nice summer.

Another of my father's brothers, my uncle Nisen, lived in a small town near Warsaw, Girardov. My mother would speak about him with affection and respect. He was a very fine person and also a very handy man. He had a beautiful handwriting in Yiddish. I remember his handwriting because for years my father kept one of his letters in a drawer. He worked for many years in his brother-in-law's flour mill in Lowicz. Unfortunately, Nisen died of pneumonia in 1928 at a relatively young age. By the time the news of his death reached my father, it was too late to get to the funeral by train. My father went by taxi from Warsaw to Lowicz, straight to the cemetery. A cousin of mine, Bronia Neiman, went with him to the funeral. They hardly made it in time for the burial. After he came back, my father sat shiva (the Jewish period of mourning) in the country, where we were spending the summer. Bronia

Neiman was the daughter of my father's sister Rifka, who was a warm, good-natured person. Bronia's youngest brother, Rubin Zinger, left for Palestine quite a few years before World War II. Another brother of theirs was Natan Zinger, who had a fine jewelry store in the non-Jewish area of Warsaw. I visited him on many occasions when I was a medical student, as his store was not far from the Anatomy Institute. He was a watchmaker, having learned his trade from our uncle Moshe, another of my father's brothers.

To complete my family history, I should mention two of my mother's brothers, my uncles Irving and Maurice, who had left home when I was still a very young child. Both of them emigrated from Poland to avoid military service in the Russian Army, which was much tougher than in any other army and lasted longer. Maurice left around 1913 for the United States, and Irving had left Poland before. Irving was in Belgium and England before arriving in the United States. He was a jeweler by trade—a diamond setter and an engraver—and could do beautiful art work in gold and jewelry. He also used to make beautiful drawings. The Warsaw School of Fine Arts, where he had been tested and offered a scholarship, had wanted to accept him, but my grandfather, as an Orthodox Jew, would not go along with that. Irving was considered to be a very good son, contributing from his work to the maintenance of the family, although most of the time my grandfather did fairly well, being in the jewelry business.

My uncle Maurice, on the other hand, was an amateur Jewish actor who went in a different direction, not being a working man and never having any trade. He had other kinds of interests, traveling and performing with various theater troupes. He enjoyed reciting in Yiddish and was well read in Yiddish literature. Irving came to Warsaw from London on a visit right before my Bar Mitzvah; I remember him taking a photo of me on the balcony of my parents' apartment. At the same time Maurice came home from New York on a visit after many years. Actually, they never would have been able to come back if the Russian government had still controlled Poland. Because Poland had become an independent country in 1918, Irving and Maurice were able to visit in 1922, a very happy event for my grandmother and the entire family.

When I turned thirteen, my parents made a Bar Mitzvah reception, which was not as common as it is nowadays. We had a three-room apartment. They emptied the living room and made a big party in the house, with a waiter and a cook and also a Jewish actor as an entertainer. (He happened to be the brother of one of our neighbors.) At that time my father had decided to change my teachers. I had been going to a cheder with a small number of pupils, where we studied Talmud (rabbinical commentary on the Hebrew Bible) with a rabbi. He had taught me a "pshetl"—a Yiddish term for a Talmudic discussion debating a problem—to be delivered during the Bar Mitzvah reception.

However, I already had started with my new teacher—a private teacher in my home—who, also wanting to contribute something to my Bar Mitzvah, taught me a speech in Hebrew. At the Bar Mitzvah reception, both teachers were among the guests. They did not know each other, and my cheder teacher did not know that I was switching. I delivered both these speeches, the Talmudic discussion (after the fish, I guess) and a little later the short speech in Hebrew which the new teacher had prepared for me.

After my Bar Mitzvah I had a tutor and then took an entrance exam to an evening commercial school in Warsaw, which I passed. I went there for two years, graduating around the age of fifteen. It was a four-year school, very well known and run by the Warsaw Merchants Organization. At the same time I was studying Talmud privately with another pupil with a rabbi in his home a few hours a day. Around fifteen or so, I discontinued most of my Talmudic studies and began taking private lessons at home in order to prepare myself for high school. My father did not care too much for this idea, being afraid that I would stop being religious. He wanted me to be satisfied with the commercial career school and expected me to join him in business. However, he went along with my plan, and for a year or two I had teachers at home, where I studied all the subjects parallel to the high school curriculum. I had very good teachers—they were good students from private Hebrew high schools in Warsaw. One of them, Kuniegis, was teaching me the secular subjects, while his father was teaching me Bible, which was also one of the required subjects at Hebrew high schools.

At seventeen I passed an entrance exam to the seventh grade in high school (called "gymnasium" in Poland), which corresponds to the eleventh grade in the United States. I attended a private Jewish high school, the director and owner of which was an engineer named Jacob Finkel. After two years, I graduated from high school in 1928 at the age of nineteen, pretty late compared with most students today. I was a good student but had started in a roundabout way, having entered school at seventeen.

## Chapter Two

# My Education After High School

In 1928 I went with my parents to the country for a summer vacation. Actually, I was with my mother, with my father coming out only for Saturdays and Sundays. We were discussing what to do next, and my father again wanted me to join him in business. At that time I had a friend from high school whose parents were well-to-do business people. This friend had decided to go to the Commercial Academy in Warsaw. Because of him and his idea my father consented to send me there too. As he wanted me to be a businessman, I convinced him that I should at least be an educated businessman.

So, in September 1928 I began at the Commercial Academy, at 6 Rakowiecka Street, which was a very modern building with a very nice auditorium. Classes were held at various hours, some even at five and six o'clock in the evening. As a matter of fact, I was going there twice a day, although it was about an hour's ride from home by trolley car each way. I was living in the Jewish area of Warsaw, which was at the opposite end of the city from the Commercial Academy. Nonetheless, traveling on the trolley was an enjoyable experience. Most of us had quarterly trolley car tickets, with the privilege of changing trolley cars at any stop, whenever we could, without paying any extra fare. We had a lot of fun, usually entering the trolley car at the rear entrance, going through to the front, and then, if there was another trolley car in front of us at the stop, jumping to that one to gain a minute.

The curriculum at the Commercial Academy was (not surprisingly) mainly commercial, including geography, economics, insurance, accounting, special arithmetic for insurance, commercial history, commercial law, and sociology. It was a school that required a lot of work and regular attendance. Tests, called colloquia, were given by the teaching assistants quite frequently. During the first two years all the students took the same subjects, but for the third year each of us had to pick a specialized field, such as the consular department, economics department, or bookkeeping-accounting department. I chose the bookkeeping-accounting department.

In order to get a diploma, after three years I had to write a thesis, on which I worked in the library, going through various journals and compiling statistics during the fourth year. The subject of my thesis was the import and export trade between Poland and Sweden. The most important product exported from Poland to Sweden was coal, while iron ore was imported to Poland from Sweden. I spent many months on this thesis, having to take different statistical material from Polish as well as Swedish journals without knowing the Swedish language, but somehow I managed to figure out these things. I spent most of this time in a beautiful and luxuriously furnished modern library building. There was a red-walled smoking room, and, although I was not smoking, I would go out there to rest a little and talk to others when I became tired of looking for hours on end at all these statistics.

I took pretty good notes during my commercial school years and usually studied by myself, only occasionally reviewing some subjects with other students. I remember some girls with whom I was not very much involved but who very much insisted that I come to study or review with them. I did not go for it, being afraid that I would become distracted from studying; I preferred to study by myself. I was not the kind of fellow who was dating, either, at that time.

I did begin dating after finishing the Commercial Academy when I was twenty-two. I remember one girl whom I met through my cousin Judith, who was a friend of hers. Because neither of us had a telephone we usually made a date from one time to the next. Once she did not come for the date, and I was quite upset; of course, looking back now it seems very silly. I did not know how to get in touch with her; one of my good friends, George Lewenson, offered to deliver a little note to her, and we got together again. But the relationship did not last too long, and some time later I ended it.

When I finished the thesis for the Commercial Academy and received the diploma from the school's rector, Mr. Miklaszewski (who had been Minister of Education in the Polish government), he was very friendly and asked me what I was intending to do. Being a Jew in Poland, I could not, even with this diploma, get the same position or job as my non-Jewish colleagues. As if not realizing that I was a Jew, he told me very nice stories about the high positions that some of our graduates had attained. The positions that they had really were very impressive at that time in Poland because the Commercial Academy was a prestigious new school, and there weren't enough people in Poland qualified in the economics field. Therefore, the graduates, except for the Jews, were offered the best positions in banking and government. I felt like letting him know my feelings in a polite way and told him that, after having graduated and rece…

not know what I could a…

The following year (193…

at the University of Warsaw…

were no limitations on the accept…

into medical school, which is wha…

As a Jew you also could get into suc…

or physics, but after graduating you coul…

of such subjects because most of the school…

possible for a Jewish teacher to get a job in a P…

of Jewish private high schools, such as the one I…

because of the relatively high tuition, which most pe…

Studying law did not require much attendance (most…

knew the professors, there were very large classes, and no…

dance), and most studies were done at home from books or…

were transcribed lectures of the professors. I passed all the exa…

two subjects which I did not study, planning to study during the s…

take the exams after the vacation. You were allowed to leave two su…

after the summer. At that time I was working part-time doing some ac…

ing for the father of a friend who had a transportation business. My frien…

classmate from the Commercial Academy, was doing the accounting for his

father, and he wanted me to help him because he had too much work. So,

while I was studying law I also was earning some money. (I had not earned

any money prior to that. During the two years of high school I did some tutor-

ing of two of my classmates in math and Latin, but I do not think that I was

paid, or if I was paid something it was not much. When I was a student at the

Commercial Academy, I was studying full-time and did not work. My father

paid the pretty high tuition—it was a private institution mostly for fairly well-

to-do people—and gave me everything that I needed for personal expenses.

There were no scholarships nor any form of tuition reduction.)

One day during the summer following the first year of law school (1933),

on the way home from work I met a classmate from high school named Szy-

frys. He also had been a good student in high school, and after high school he

had attended the University of Warsaw's law school, graduating from there

at the same time that I had graduated from the Commercial Academy. I am

describing my conversation with him because it had a very decisive effect

on my future life. He told me that he had decided, after having graduated

from law school, to try to get into medical school so that he could be a legal

expert in court on medical problems, in other words, to specialize in forensic

medicine. I always had wanted to get into medical school, but it was very

difficult for a Jew in Poland to do so. Some people managed to get in with

ved this diploma, I was going to study law since I did

complish with this diploma.

) I actually did apply to and began studying law

law school, one of the schools where there

nce of Jews. Many Jews who could not get

I had wanted originally, went into law.

departments as history, mathematics,

I not accomplish much as a teacher

were state run and it was hardly

olish state school. The number

had attended, were limited

ople could not afford.

of the students hardly

ody checked atten-

"scripts," which

ms except the

ummer and

iects for

ount-

a

)uld
ical
me
of
)ne
)le
of
ut
)e

...... mention, while discussing the ...... of Warsaw, that the Jews of Warsaw had a type of limited self-government known as the Jewish Community Board of Warsaw. This board ran some religious and trade schools, as well as some welfare agencies for the Jewish people. It also was in charge of the Jewish cemetery, which was a big source of income for the Jewish community government. When a rich person died, the board would bargain with the family, demanding a substantial price for a burial lot, and the family of the deceased had no choice. The board had the power to collect some taxes from the Jewish members of the community and handed over unpaid taxes for collection to the general tax authorities, who collected them for the Jewish community. These taxes were actually minimal compared to the general taxes all citizens—Jews and non-Jews—paid. The general tax for each business was based on that business's total turnover, that is, on the gross volume of business done by that businessperson. In the absence of reliable accounting books, the amount of business for each taxpayer was estimated by special committees, becoming a source of great abuse. Although this was a general tax, paid by all citizens, not only Jews, the tax collectors were more zealous to collect from Jews than from other citizens, always complaining that the Jews were cheating and not reporting enough income.

When I was born, Poland had been divided for more than a century into three parts as a result of conquests by Austria, Russia, and Germany. The central part with the capital of Warsaw was called Congress Poland, which had been established by an international congress and was under Russian occupation. The official language was Russian, although there were many Polish schools and Polish was spoken. When World War I broke out in 1914, the citizens—Jews and non-Jews—were drafted by the Russian Army. At the end of the war, in 1918, Poland emerged as an independent country after a brief period of German occupation. Then nine years old, I remember young Polish boys in Polish Army uniforms (the nucleus of the future Polish Army) disarming German soldiers in the street, taking away their weapons and letting them walk away. During the German occupation of Poland, the Jews, speaking Yiddish (a combined derivative of Hebrew and German), communicated quite well with the Germans, in contrast to the Poles, and took advantage of various business opportunities.

Let me now return to my situation in 1933, when my friend Szyfrys and I went to see the secretary of the dean of the medical school concerning our possibilities for admission. By applying under the usual set of rules, including the entrance exam, we never would have gotten in, simply because we were Jews. The secretary told us that there was a possibility that for one year the school would try to accept anybody who already had an academic diploma and not make them take the entrance exam, provided that there were not too many candidates. The two of us applied and kept it a secret. I did not tell my parents, at least not my father. One day, my friend Szyfrys called up my father in the store (we had no telephone at home) and told him, "You know, your son was accepted into medical school." My father did not know from anything. But when I explained it to him, he was very happy because business had not been very good for a few years and he knew that I did not really care for the business.

It is difficult to describe, compared to present-day circumstances, what an event it was for a Jewish boy or girl to be accepted to a medical school at a university in Poland. Many of us wanted to study medicine, and whoever could afford it had to go abroad to France, Italy, or other countries. This was possible only if the parents wanted and could afford it. Some went even when their parents could not afford it. Along with trying to learn the language of the particular country, they struggled to find work; it was quite a hardship. Then, when they came back to Poland with their diploma, they had to repeat all their exams. The Polish government did not make it easy for them, as it took a year or two before they even were admitted to take all these exams. The medical schools abroad were probably as good as, if not better than, the schools in Poland, but the Polish government made it difficult for the Jews in every possible way.

The reason why many of the young Jewish people were anxious to get into medicine was that there were not many other professions open to Jews. One could not accomplish much as a teacher, nor could one get a job with a large institution, firm, or bank, and certainly not a government job. The only occupation left was business or a trade, for which people with education did not care much. Everybody tried to be in an independent profession where he or she would be on his or her own, and there were only a few choices—to be a doctor, lawyer, or dentist. Dentistry was just as difficult to get into as medicine. It was easy for Jewish students to get into the law school at the University of Warsaw or another Polish university. However, there was still another step required in order to become a lawyer–an apprenticeship. At first, work with an established lawyer was sufficient for the apprenticeship. Later on, work in court, as a clerk, for a few years (two, I believe) was required to be admitted to practice law. It was difficult to get such a clerkship. When a Jewish graduate became a lawyer, there were limited opportunities compared with non-Jewish lawyers, mainly private practice. Because there were large numbers of Jewish lawyers, many of them went into something else (such as real estate), being unable to make a living practicing law.

Besides the approximately 120 students who were accepted every year to the University of Warsaw's medical school, there were a number of military medical students, who were exclusively non-Jewish. They were in army uniforms; the Polish Army paid for their education, and they were obligated to be in military medicine for a few years after graduation.

The medical curriculum was two years of basic studies followed by four years of clinical studies. It started with physics and chemistry, with exams after the first year, and other subjects (anatomy, histology, embryology, physiology) with final exams after two years. Following this, the next four years involved mostly clinical subjects—lectures and work with patients in hospitals. The most vivid impression that stays in my mind was the first day in the anatomicum (the dissection room) as we walked in to work on the cadavers. There were six students assigned to each cadaver, lying on a marble table, with each pair of students assigned a different part of the body. The first year we had to dissect the muscles, after taking off the skin. I remember one incident from this work. I was working with another student on an arm which had quite a bit of fat under the skin. We were supposed to take off the skin first, very carefully, without taking any fat along with the skin. As this required a lot of time, we thought that we could be smart and get away with removing the fat and the skin at the same time in order to get to the muscles. We were caught on this and had to do the whole arm over. Also, I never will forget the orderly, or attendant, of this anatomicum, who was in charge of the cadavers. He had to put the cadavers away after work in a big basin with Formalin (a formaldehyde solution) and put them back on the same table before the next session.

## Chapter Three

# Marriage and Family

Despite having a lot of work and studying to do in medical school and not having been previously much involved in social life, together with my classmate Szyfrys and other friends I helped organize a Jewish Academic Literary Artistic Club. The name sounds impressive, but actually we just wanted to have a little fun. I do not remember how we managed financially, although I was the treasurer. We rented a large hall in the center of Warsaw, in the Theater Square, near the opera and all the theaters. There we had lectures, dances, and meetings. We had quite a big crowd of students, not only from the medical school but also from other academic schools in Warsaw.

At one of these club events I met my future wife, Helen Rosenfein, who was a graduate of the Commercial Academy, the same one from which I had graduated in 1932. She had graduated a year later than me, but I had never met her at the Commercial Academy. We began dating. Usually I would meet her on Saturday evenings at the other end of Warsaw because she was taking English language courses there. I got there by trolley car. We would take a long walk for a couple of hours on the way home. It was winter, but we did not mind. We became more friendly, but I did not have much time to go out, so she would meet me when I was leaving my anatomicum classes. We would go home by trolley car, enjoying each other's company on this one-hour trip. She frequently would rewrite my notes from classes to make it easier for me later when I had to study for exams. Once she mentioned that, when she had read the previous year's list of students accepted to medical school (a friend of hers had been accepted that year, too) and had come across my name, she had not thought that I was a Jew. My last name was Gliniewiecki (purely Polish), but I still could not understand why she did not know that I was Jewish because my first name was Hersz, which was more of a Jewish than Polish name.

We became very friendly, but still I was not invited to her home for quite some time. Things were different than nowadays, and you had to be going out for a very long time before you addressed each other on a first-name basis. The second summer after we had met, her parents rented a bungalow in a suburban place for the summer season. I somehow convinced my parents to also rent a little summer place in the same area so that we could be together during the summer.

Despite my being only a third-year medical student, we decided to get married. She was an only child, and her parents were very well off and had quite a large apartment. We thought that we could just get married and have a room in their apartment; this would be enough for my student years. I asked her parents, and they accepted my proposal. After that I began visiting their home quite regularly. Usually after I finished my evening studying, I would visit Helen and then we, together with her parents, would have our dairy meal at about eight in the evening. I used to spend a lot of time at the table talking with her father, whom I admired. He was a very friendly and well-read man. They used to take books from the library and usually exchange them for other books after a day or two. Helen would read them during the day, and her father would read them late at night. He was very pleasant, intelligent, and good-natured–a truly fine person.

My budget was quite limited. At that time I was working as a salaried general secretary of the Jewish Medical Student Organization, which was separate from the non-Jewish Medical Student Organization. The Jewish students from all the other schools of the university had one organization jointly, but we Jewish medical students had our own separate organization. I worked there a few evenings a week. It was a very active organization recognized by the School of Medicine and the university as the representative of the Jewish students. The organization provided financial help to some students of limited means and also dispensed reduced-priced tickets to out-of-town students for dinners in the kitchen of the general Jewish Student Organization of the university. Most of the money for this was raised by the organization itself, as there was hardly any subsidy from the university or anywhere else. We held our own events, which were very popular and a source of income. Girls liked to come to these affairs, hoping to meet a future doctor. We had a very well-publicized summer camp in a resort on the Baltic Sea, where any student (not only medical ones) could spend a month. This was a hot season of work for me, as I was taking care of the organization's financial aspects, preparing final lists of the campers and payments, and sending the lists out to the camp manager with the last train around midnight before the people were to arrive. This camp was one of the organization's main sources of income.

Whatever I earned was adequate for my personal needs. I did not feel like taking from my father and certainly not from my father-in-law. Helen was getting some money from her father; we were planning to live on a very thrifty budget when married. We married in the beginning of September 1936. It was stylish for students not to have a big wedding, even though their parents wanted one. They would be married in their sports clothes by a rabbi, with a couple of close friends and family present, and then go on their honeymoon. Our parents, and in particular my future father-in-law, were pleading with us, as they each had only one child and wanted to have a wedding. We went along with this but refused to have a large wedding in a special hall with music. We had quite a nice reception in my in-laws' apartment, without music. A rabbi came and performed the ceremony, and then there was a nice dinner for members of our families.

For our honeymoon we went to a resort place, Krynica, and both sets of parents came to see us off at the main railroad station. It was a very popular and nice resort area in southern Poland, with baths, mineral waters, and luxurious hotels with entertainment. One of the best-known hotels was Patria, owned by the Polish opera star, John Keipura, who had built it for his parents. There were only two big, nice kosher hotels in Krynica. One was Frankel's, and the other, where we stayed, was Kryniczanka. There we spent a few weeks over the Jewish holidays. I still remember how beautifully the holidays were observed there; of course, there were Jewish services. Among the prominent guests was a senator of the Polish Parliament, Salo Budzyner, who was a Levi (a Jew descended from the tribe of Levi, for whom certain religious functions were reserved), like myself. He got an "aliyah" (being called up to the Torah) on the first day of Rosh Hashanah (the Jewish New Year), and I got one on the second day. For Rosh Hashanah evening dinner after services the tables were beautifully decorated with chocolates and colorful ribbons at every setting, with everybody dressed up as if they were going to a wedding. It was very impressive.

After our honeymoon, life went back to its daily routine, to studying. We did not plan to have children, but things happen and Helen became pregnant. On the third of May 1937 (May 3 is a Polish national holiday celebrating the Polish constitution), we were walking with one of Helen's girlfriends on Marszalkowska Street (one of the main streets in Warsaw) when a young Polish hooligan hit me in the back; I think that Helen fell on the street. She had a miscarriage after this. We actually were trying not to have a child until I graduated, but my father-in-law was pleading with us to have a child, as he was very anxious to have a grandchild. He said to us, "You just give birth to the child and I'll take care of everything." He later kept his word—he was a wonderful man in many respects. Helen became pregnant again, and a son,

Alexander Sholom, was born on October 18, 1938, which was Simhat Torah (the Jewish holiday marking the completion of the annual cycle of reading the Torah). He was delivered in a private obstetrical hospital by a Dr. Fryszberg (whose daughter Halina happened to be my classmate in medical school). I remember walking home with my father-in-law from the hospital the morning after the delivery—we were both very happy.

The following summer, which was the summer of 1939, before the outbreak of World War II, my in-laws rented a three-room summer bungalow in the same suburb where they had been a few years before. Helen was there with her parents and the baby, and I was studying for my exams at home in Warsaw. I had taken some final exams prior to that. After finishing all of my studies in June 1939, I was preparing for the remaining final exams in the fall and was coming out to the country for weekends.

My father-in-law owned in partnership with one of his brothers a nice apartment building in the city (#8 Ciepla Street), which gave him substantial income. Besides this he was managing another apartment building owned by one of his tenants. Between the two buildings he did not work very hard, usually just a few hours every day, commuting to the summer place. He had time to read, take it easy, and enjoy his grandchild.

During that summer there already was talk of impending war. It was after Hitler's anschluss (annexation) of Austria and occupation of the Sudetenland (part of Czechoslovakia), both in 1938. Poland was being threatened, though not yet officially. At that time in New York, the World's Fair was taking place, and I had an idea to leave for New York as a tourist for the World's Fair with Helen and Alexander, thinking of my two uncles in New York, Irving and Maurice. My mother, as well as my in-laws, objected to this, and, besides, it was too complicated. We just became passive like all the other people, as if waiting for the tragedy to develop. Immigration to the United States was limited, regulated by a quota according to country of birth. So the people who tried to get to America had a long waiting list, and then they needed an affidavit from someone living in the United States who was willing to support them. It would have been impossible to emigrate through these normal channels, which is why we thought we would come as tourists to New York and in some way manage to stay there. It did not work out anyway.

*Chapter Four*

# The Outbreak of War and the Flight East

That summer of 1939, while my family was still in the country and I was in the city, there were already preparations for the defense of Warsaw. Many men, including myself, were voluntarily going to the suburbs around Warsaw, digging trenches in the hope that this would be important for the defense against the Germans. I should mention my military classification, 1A, fit for service; by a lucky coincidence I was not called. Most Jews, particularly the educated ones, were not called to serve in the Polish Army because, according to military regulations, the army would have to give us an officer's rank, which it did not care to do. We were considered to be above the required contingent (quota), which meant that the army had enough soldiers to meet its needs, so a certain number of men were just not called. In case of war, everybody had to be ready to be called. However, in peacetime they called every physician, even Jewish ones, so I would be called as soon as I graduated from medical school. I had not yet completed my exams, having a few left which I was going to take after September, at the beginning of the new school year, but on September 1, 1939, the war broke out.

My family already had returned in a hurry to Warsaw, as did all the other people from the suburban country places. On Friday, September 1, while walking on the street we heard the piercing sounds of the sirens. Nobody realized that this was a true alarm, as we had had many test alarms before. We also had made black window shades to use in case of a night air raid and had pasted the window panes with paper strips to protect them from breaking in case of bombing. As I look back on all this, it seems quite childish. The German Army was much better equipped and more mechanized than the Polish Army, which was famous for its infantry but was not very technically advanced. Besides, there was no adequate defense against the German air raids.

When the war broke out, the national anthem was played over the Polish radio, and there was a speech by the chief commander of the Polish Armed Forces, General Rydz Smigly. He finished this speech with the famous words, "We will not even give a button from our uniforms, we will fight." The confidence was based on a defense treaty with Great Britain and an old alliance with France dating back to World War I. I remember a big parade when I was a youngster, after World War I, when Marshall Foch from France visited Warsaw, and all the main streets were decorated with Polish and French flags. Now, at the outbreak of World War II, Poland's treaty with Great Britain was emphasized over the Polish radio, where the British anthem was played repeatedly. We were sure that we would be able to resist the Germans with the support of these two allies. As it turned out, Germany invaded Poland along the entire frontier and moved quite rapidly. This brings to my mind a sad episode which had taken place a year or more before the outbreak of the war. Germany had been throwing out Polish Jewish citizens who had resided for many years in Germany, sending them back to Poland, which refused to accept them. There was a whole group of these people living in horrible conditions in a camp-like setting near the frontier, around the town of Zbonszyn. They had no home in Germany and no home in Poland. It was a tragic situation for these people, who were living on public support from the Jewish community.

It did not take the Germans long to overrun Poland from the west to the east. As the German Army was moving, the Polish people were running, especially the Jews, who knew what to expect from Hitler's Germany. All the roads toward the east were crowded with men of all ages walking or, if lucky, on horse and wagon. The whole country became one big chaos in a few days.

It should be noted that Poland had many German nationals, "volksdeutsche," as they were called in German, who had lived in Poland for generations. As a matter of fact, the textile industry was to a large degree in German nationals' hands, although there were also some Jews and Poles in this industry. This brings to mind a Mr. Schmidt, one of my father-in-law's tenants in the house which he managed. A German national who had moved in only about a year or so prior to the outbreak of the war, he later turned out to have been a German spy who was working and preparing the groundwork for the Germans. As soon as the Germans occupied various towns, these German nationals would take over the local government under the direction of the Germans.

On Wednesday, September 6, there was a call over the Polish radio that all men able to bear arms should leave Warsaw and go toward the east of Poland, where a resistance would be put up. When this call came, I left my home. I already had said good-bye to my parents, as I had been planning the day before to join the Polish Army voluntarily, knowing that I would be drafted anyway. Being a graduate medical student, missing only a few exams to graduation, I expected to get some type of medical rank. I did not realize that the dangers would be just the same for a doctor as for any soldier. That evening I left Warsaw with my father-in-law, his brother, and the brother's two sons. The five of us left Warsaw, not realizing what we were getting into. We expected to get some sort of transportation, but as soon as we had walked ten blocks we found that there were no trolley cars. Everything was being used to make barricades, so we just walked the streets until we came to the roads leading out of Warsaw. There we met hundreds and thousands of men, walking and walking, without any goal, any destination, just walking out of Warsaw without any luggage. I had a briefcase that contained a towel and some personal things. I thought that when I would reach a military hospital I would join voluntarily.

It would take endless time and space to describe this trip. We were exhausted walking. We did not have a car; very few people did, and those who did had to leave them, pushing the cars into a ditch on the road because they could not get any gasoline. Then they would just start walking with all the others. Money is usually helpful, and in some places we were lucky and hired someone with a horse and wagon to transport us, moving at about twenty kilometers (about 12.4 miles) an hour. In one of these little towns in which we stayed overnight, with many other people around, we had something to eat. The townspeople had baked bread, which we were very happy to get, along with something to drink. Then we moved on again like this for several days.

On one occasion the five of us somehow managed to get on a fire engine from the fire department of the town of Lowicz. I was hanging on and standing on this open fire engine like a flagpole, racing through the roads. This was a big accomplishment, instead of having to walk or go a couple of kilometers by horse and wagon and then having to change to another horse and wagon or walk again. We got quite ahead with this fire engine.

While we were walking, running, or riding eastward on the roads, the German airplanes were roaring about without any resistance and sometimes lowering themselves over our heads, forcing us to run into the fields to hide in the crops. They could have shot us all out, but I guess this was not their purpose and we did not mean anything to them. It was frightening; we were tired, hungry, and thirsty. When we saw a farm from a distance, we would walk off the road to buy something to eat.

One Saturday afternoon we reached the town of Brest-Litovsk (its Russian name, as it used to belong to Russia). It was a very big military center in Poland, with one of the largest military hospitals. Planning to report there for military service, I started to inquire about this hospital and was told that it, too, was being evacuated. Actually, the entire military establishment was falling apart. We walked into a stranger's home, like everybody else did; everyone was very hospitable. I started to take a shower, but, soon after, air raid sirens sounded, and we had to run to the shelter, which was in the basement of the house. I was a little delayed getting to the shelter because I had to get dressed. I looked across the street from the bathroom window and saw the building across the road coming down. Luckily, the building that we were in was not damaged, and the bombing alarm was soon over. The town had been bombed for only a few minutes, and, by the time I got to the basement, the air raid was over.

The next day, Sunday morning, many of the Jewish people of Brest-Litovsk started to leave the town, and we decided to leave as well. My father-in-law, his brother, the brother's two sons, and I stayed together wherever we went. We walked or got a ride until we reached the next town, Kobryn. I had left home without a hat, and in Kobryn I bought a beret. I had never worn a beret in my life before, but I thought that this would be a good thing to have because you also can sleep in it, it does not occupy much space (as a hat does), and you can put it in your pocket. In Kobryn I also got a shave and a haircut in a barber shop.

The next day we kept on moving until we got to Pinsk, which was a big town. I knew some people from this town who had attended the Commercial Academy in Warsaw. At the time that I got there, though, the whole town was in such a chaotic state that it did not matter whom you knew or where you went. We could not remain there either, as there was no place to stay or sleep, but we could not go much further because we already were close to the eastern frontier of Poland, not far from the Russian border.

We kept on going until we got to a smaller town, Luniniec, where we stayed for a few days. We now were close to our "Russian friends;" as Jews we were much less afraid of the Russians than of the Germans. We thought of Russia as a place where there was justice and equality for everyone and no discrimination against the Jews, which we found out later was a fantasy. In Luniniec we found many people, crowds of people, who had come from all over Poland. People could not go any further, so the place was overcrowded. I remember spending the first night in the house of a man selling Polish government lottery tickets. In Poland there was a government lottery with many drawings during the year. The people selling these tickets were licensed to do so by the government. They had to pay a fee to the government and made a commission from selling the tickets. As an official sign of his business, the man had on the wall a framed picture of the President of Poland, Moscicki, and another picture of the Polish eagle. The funny part of it was that, when people would come in bringing news and gossip that the

Russians were approaching from the other side, he quickly would remove the two pictures, but an hour later, when someone else came in and said that it was just a rumor, he would hang the pictures back up.

We stayed in this town around the time of Yom Kippur (the Day of Atonement, the most solemn Jewish holiday), September 23, and rented a place to live, the empty apartment of a Jewish family. I believe that the husband of this family had joined the army and his wife and children had gone to live with her mother. We managed to buy some potatoes and meat, and my father-in-law and his brother did the cooking. We ate before the Yom Kippur fast and went for Kol Nidre (the opening prayer) services to the local synagogue, where we spent the evening and all of the next day.

We felt comfortable at that time with the Russian Army, which had arrived and was occupying the town. There were a number of Jewish soldiers in the Russian Army. They were very friendly to us, communicating in Yiddish. There was a joke going around about their advice to us that "we should not worry, we always would get enough work to do, we would earn a living, but we would not lick any honey," meaning that we hardly would earn a living and we would not live in luxury. And, besides, they warned us not to become involved in any politics. In brief, "just work and eat what you can and do not mix into politics."

I should mention that Germany had started the war with Poland after the German Foreign Minister, von Ribbentrop, had signed a nonaggression treaty (the Molotov-Ribbentrop Pact) with Russia. Russia apparently promised not to fight the Germans, and the two countries decided to divide Poland between themselves. Germany moved eastward and Russia westward through Poland. Although the Germans were moving eastward past Warsaw, they did not occupy Warsaw itself for about three or four weeks because of the heroic resistance which the city put up. The Germans were bombing Warsaw, destroying many buildings and forcing the people to the shelters (basements) during air raids for the three or four weeks until they surrendered.

So we found ourselves under Russian occupation. The Russians who occupied the eastern part of Poland disarmed all the Polish officers and soldiers who had not managed to get out of their uniforms and took them as prisoners of war. Later, it became apparent that they had killed thousands of Polish officers at Katyn (a forest) near the city of Smolensk and had put the blame on the Germans, who occupied the area later when they overran Russia in 1941. The Russians did not bother the civilian population, and people moved about freely.

About the time of the Jewish holiday of Sukkoth, September 28, we went to Bialystok, a very large district town with a sizable Jewish population. It was one of the centers of the Polish textile industry. There the five of us lived with a Jewish family. It was impossible to buy anything, as the stores were quickly emptied out. Apparently people were hoarding things, and, when merchandise was delivered, it would be sold out in a hurry; people were standing in lines for goods. I was in my summer shoes, I had no rubbers, winter was approaching, and I did not have any winter clothes. A young lady, the daughter of the people with whom we were staying, happened to know "somebody," and she went with me to a store where I got a pair of rubbers. The Russian soldiers gave the civilians some menial jobs in exchange for food or money, and the older of my two cousins took advantage of this opportunity.

In the meantime Warsaw had surrendered to the Germans. My father-in-law and his brother thought that the brother's sons and I should not go back home to the Nazi occupation, expecting some kind of atrocities, which later unfortunately became a reality. However, they felt that no matter what would happen they should go home to be with their wives and children. My father-in-law had left his wife and his daughter (my wife), along with our one-year-old child. My father-in-law's brother had left his wife and two unmarried daughters, the older a dentist and the younger a teenager.

Going back home meant sneaking through the new border established between the Germans and the Russians. However, the Russian soldiers who were spread all along the frontier did not make it difficult at that time for people to go from one side to another. This was not a clearly planned kind of trip by train. My father-in-law and his brother started out on their way back to Warsaw from Bialystok without knowing what kind of route or what modes of transportation they would be using until they got home or if they would get home safely at all. My father-in-law hoped that, as I was missing only a few of my final exams, I would get my diploma and settle as a physician under the Russians. Under this "wonderful Russian paradise" we expected to have a decent life, especially with my having a good profession. He hoped that somehow Helen and Alexander would join me and that perhaps we all would be together in the not-too-distant future. This was his dream and my dream. With tears in his eyes, he left us, going home, not sure if he would ever make it.

After the fathers left, my older cousin (Jacob) went his own way. I do not know much about what happened to him, but two years later we met again in the Warsaw ghetto. My younger cousin, Solomon, who was about seventeen, remained with me. I was anxious to get to some kind of a university town to complete my exams and obtain my diploma. Leaving Solomon I went to Vilna, which was in northeastern Poland. There was a Polish university there which at the time of my arrival was functioning under the Russian occupation. In Vilna I stayed and lived fairly comfortably with Harry Orenstein, who was my mother-in-law's youngest brother. His family had a nice apartment in a very exclusive area of Vilna. I recall that in the same house lived the senator from Vilna, Senator Prystor. His name was infamously remembered by the Jews because he had introduced a law in the Polish Senate that forbade ritual slaughter for kosher meat for Jews. I got in touch with the Jewish student medical organization and a group of other graduate students planning to take the exams in Vilna.

In the meantime, the frontiers were becoming more closed and more difficult to cross. Rumors began to spread that Vilna would be included in Lithuania and therefore be under Lithuanian authorities, although occupied by the Russians. At that time there were many people from Warsaw and all over Poland in Vilna who, in contrast to myself, did not have to take exams or get a diploma. Most of them gladly remained in Vilna, hoping that it would become part of Lithuania. They thought that it would be easier to get out from Lithuania to go to other countries, even outside Europe. As I found out later, a friend from Warsaw, Shilem Warhaftig, and his family also were in Vilna. They were able to get to Kovno (the capital of Lithuania) and from there traveled all the way through Russia. They reached Shanghai and in that way eventually got to Israel. I know that Harry Orenstein, along with his wife and two boys, also traveled all across Russia and ended up in Shanghai, as did another friend of mine, Joseph Rubinstein. Thus, a large number of Polish Jews came to spend the war years in Shanghai.

I could not think of getting away from Poland. I was by myself and had an obligation to Helen, Alexander, and my parents in Warsaw. I was afraid that if I stayed in Vilna I might have problems taking my exams and that if the authorities closed off the frontiers I might not be able to get out to go to my family or even to other Russian-occupied territories in Poland. I decided to leave Vilna and go to Lwow (also known as Lvov in Russian), in Russian-occupied southeastern Poland, where there also was a university. Also, Henry Rosenfein, who was my wife's uncle, lived in Lwow. On the way from Vilna to Lwow I spent one or more nights in Luniniec, one of the towns where we had stayed when going east. By coincidence I met my cousin Solomon there, and we both decided to go to Lwow because Henry Rosenfein was his uncle as well. It was a long trip, and we had to travel by train. Trains were running but quite irregularly; one never knew when they would arrive or where they were going. In November 1939, about two months after having left home in Warsaw, we finally arrived in Lwow and got to the home of Henry Rosenfein.

Henry Rosenfein was the youngest of my father-in-law's three brothers. His wife, Matilda, was the daughter of their oldest brother (that is, he had married his niece). They had one boy, Alexander, who was around fourteen. My uncle was an exceptionally bright man—the director of a bank in Lwow, a good bridge player, and a socialite. When we arrived there, however, there was no bank, no business, no income. The Rosenfeins were living off of their savings, and food was not abundant. It was very simple food, bread and soup and the like. They were the nicest people you could imagine, sharing with us their limited food, which at that time was very precious. The Rosenfeins lived in a beautiful apartment in a luxurious area of Lwow near Lwow's Polytechnic School. They made sleeping arrangements for us and went out of their way to accommodate us comfortably. I slept on a bed or sofa with Solomon, Matilda slept on another sofa, and Henry and his son slept in their regular bedroom.

Being of school age, Solomon entered school in Lwow. I contacted some friends who were in Lwow at that time and who also had to finish some exams in order to get their diplomas. We studied together, passed our exams, and received our diplomas on June 10, 1940.

The five or six months of my final exam studies were full of tension as far as general life in Lwow was concerned. The Russians were sending people to Siberia, especially the ones (like myself and many others) who were not permanent residents of Lwow. One morning when I walked out, the streets were full of Russian security police, in their blue uniforms and blue caps. Wherever you turned you found one and felt surrounded by them. They were walking into apartments and rounding up people who did not have a local resident passport. The Russian police just loaded them into trains supposedly taking them to some kind of labor camp, but it actually was to Siberia. They had another trick, saying that they wanted to register the people who wished to return to their families in Warsaw or to any other location in the German-occupied areas of Poland. To register or not was quite a dilemma. We finally found out that the Russian authorities were not that straightforward and that this might be a ruse to find out who was not a resident. We were afraid that, instead of sending us to Warsaw, they might send us to Siberia. Not wanting to take this chance, I did not register to go to Warsaw.

In the same building where I was living with the Rosenfeins, my father-in-law's aunt—an older lady who was a teacher from Lublin—was staying in another apartment. Like us, she had escaped from Nazi-occupied Poland, arriving in Lwow with her only daughter and son-in-law. One night this old lady was taken away to Siberia and never heard from again. Her daughter, Maryla, and son-in-law, Maurice Weis, happened to be away when the old lady was rounded up. They tried to get the mother back when the trains were being loaded but were not successful.

For quite a few nights I was sleeping in different places—one night in a furniture factory, another night in a barber shop. Trying to avoid deportation, we all were afraid to sleep in the places we were staying. There was another man, a cousin of Matilda, staying with us in the Rosenfeins' home. He was a socialist or communist and was very happy that he was living in an area under Russian occupation. He got himself a very fine job in one of the factories. As it turned out later, the Russians did not trust any Polish or Jewish communists and considered them Trotskyites. They were deported to Siberia along with the rest.

In Lwow there also were many non-Jewish Polish people who had ended up there for various reasons. Most of these Poles were trying to return home, while the Jews were trying to escape from the Nazi regime. There were a lot of black market dealings going on between the people (both Jews and non-Jews) and the Russian soldiers. Those not having businesses or jobs anymore were trying to make some money whatever way they could. The Russian soldiers, not having much at home, were anxious to buy whatever type of watch or piece of junk they could get, paying with their rubles. With these rubles you could get food in the stores whenever it was available, but it was not easy to buy a loaf of bread or any food. If there was a rumor of an expected delivery at a store, people would line up at three or four in the cold winter morning, standing on line until the stores opened at seven. As I was in Lwow from November 1939 until August 1940, I remember well these lines in the winter. In our extended Rosenfein family we all shared our duties and would alternate standing in the early morning lines. The food was not rationed, but it was sold in limited quantities per person.

The same problem existed with regard to clothing. Although the local population had enough clothes, refugees such as myself, who had no winter clothes, were trying to buy something, and this was quite expensive and difficult. I really wanted—almost as if in a dream—to get a pair of shoes and have them waterproofed because I had only the summer shoes in which I had left home in September.

In June 1940 I got my diploma from the Academy of Medicine (the name of the medical school in Lwow), signed by Professor Muzika. It was written in the Ukranian language, as the entire southeastern part of Poland, now occupied by the Russians, had become part of the Ukraine and was referred to as the western Ukraine. I do not remember when, how, and for what reason I had this diploma translated into German by an authorized translator. Apparently I thought that this would be of value if I were to go back into a German-occupied area at some future time.

According to Russian law, which was then the ruling law, after graduation a new physician was sent out by the authorities to a small, sometimes distant community to fill the position of physician. He or she did not have much of a choice where to settle, serving the community and receiving "a fair salary" paid by the government. However, I found out that some special courses for graduates were being offered and that I could become a specialist. One of these was organized by the Institute of Dermatology of the University of Charkov (in the Ukraine). A group of professors came to Lwow and gave a course in dermatology and venereal diseases. After completing this two-month course, I was certified as a specialist in dermatology and venereal diseases and sent to the district town of Tarnopol for assignment by the doctor in charge to my actual place of work.

# Chapter Five

# A Physician Under the Russians

I was assigned to a fairly big town, Skalat. There Dr. Frederick Sas, who was in charge of this local district, had to find a position for me. Previously he had been a district physician during the Polish times and now had this same function under the Russians. The town had a mixed population—Ukrainians, Poles, and a fair number of Jews. There was a nice-size hospital, and the nurses were actually nuns who had replaced their habits, which were not welcomed by the Russians, with regular nurses' uniforms. Most of the town's doctors were affiliated with the hospital, and, although private medical care was still available to the population by the local doctors who had their offices, this was rather limited. The practice of medicine was centered in a public dispensary and in the hospital.

There was supposed to be a doctor on call in the hospital 24 hours a day. Because none of the practicing doctors already there liked having such duty, it was very convenient for them to have me around there. I did not have any clothes, furniture, apartment, or anything, so they were "very generous" and set me up in the hospital with room and board in exchange for duty. Actually, it was not 24-hour duty, occurring mostly in the late afternoon and at night. From eight in the morning until one in the afternoon, I was working in the dispensary in my new specialty of skin and venereal diseases. I lived in the hospital, ate in the hospital, and was on night duty at the hospital.

In the dispensary I worked with another Jewish refugee doctor, Dr. Henry Fey from Katowice. He also had had to get away from a Nazi-occupied area, Upper Silesia. Dr. Fey, an experienced physician, was in charge of the skin and venereal diseases clinic, and I, just out of school, was the junior physician under him. He was very nice to me, and I learned much from him. We had many patients with skin diseases and some with venereal diseases. From patients who had gonorrhea we would take smears, staining and examining them right there under the microscope. I became quite efficient under his direction in the diagnosis and treatment of these diseases. The treatment of venereal diseases was quite old-fashioned and not as brief and simple as it is now. There was no penicillin at that time, and, although sulpha drugs were starting to come out, they were not yet available to us. The patients had to return for daily irrigations with potassium permanganate solution, and we would check their smears each day until they were cured.

After some time I managed to give up my job at the hospital and decided to live on the salary that I was getting as a skin and venereal diseases specialist at the dispensary. I rented a furnished room with a family named Wachtel, whose nephew, Dr. Phillip Sommerstein, I had met in the dispensary. Dr. Sommerstein was working in the same building as I but in a different capacity, being the public health physician from Skalat. (After the war he came to the United States, settling in Pittsburgh.) With the Wachtels I had a beautiful, large room, but in the winter, with no heat and no coal, it was quite freezing there. Also, the houses in Skalat had no indoor toilet facilities and no running water; every house had an outside well. Mrs. Wachtel was very friendly, sitting and chatting sometimes with me in the evening in the large warm kitchen. I remember her telling me stories from World War I about Vienna, where she had spent quite some time temporarily away from her permanent residence.

I had about adjusted to my situation in Skalat and was getting along very well with Dr. Fey and with a practical nurse, a young lady from Warsaw, who was assigned to our clinic. I even had some private patients and a few extra rubles, which I used to have a pair of good high leather boots made for me. Then suddenly one day I received an order from the district that I was being transferred to a large village named Germakowka, located in the southeasternmost corner of Poland, not far from the border with Romania. I was given a few days' time before having to leave. With tears in my eyes, I parted from the Wachtel family and from the people with whom I was working.

My instructions from the district health officer were that I was to travel by train to a station called Ivanie Puste, where he would be waiting to take me to Germakowka. This station was the last stop on this line. Its name, Ivanie Puste, well described it. "Puste" means "empty," and there was actually nothing there but the little station building. I arrived at Ivanie Puste with my valise. There the district heath officer, a big husky Ukrainian, waited for me. In about an hour or so we arrived by horse and wagon at the next town, Mielnica. In Mielnica I slept overnight in the small hotel where my Ukrainian boss had taken me. The next morning we went to Germakowka, where I was supposed to be practicing as the only physician.

There actually was a physician there already, a Ukrainian native of that village, Dr. Aksenteev. Because he was a native Ukrainian he was advancing to another job in a bigger town, and I was to take his place. When I arrived in Germakowka, the Ukrainian boss took me to Dr. Aksenteev. Knowing that I was Jewish, he set me up with a Jewish family named Raab, who lived in a nice house on the main road. Besides Mr. and Mrs. Raab, there were their two daughters, a young son, and Mrs. Raab's elderly mother. I was assigned to a newly organized dispensary, with daily office hours from eight in the morning until one in the afternoon, treating free of charge patients with all kinds of problems as in a general family practice. After office hours I was on call 24 hours a day, making house calls not only in Germakowka but also in the entire area within a radius of fifteen or twenty kilometers, being picked up by a farmer in his horse and wagon whenever one needed me.

In the meantime the general situation had settled down a little. I was corresponding with my family in Warsaw. It was not permitted to write any letters but only open postcards. To fit as much as I could on a postcard I would write in very tiny letters. I also corresponded with my relatives in Lwow with whom I had been staying. One day, much to my surprise, I received a piece of mail from Komi S.S.R., one of the northeastern areas of Russia. It was from my friend George Lewenson, who also had been in Brest-Litovsk but had been taken away from there when the Russians were sending people to Siberia. Somehow he had found out where I was, and we then were able to maintain some contact by mail.

I was fairly well set up in Germakowka, and, besides, I did not need much. Food was plentiful in these small villages, and farmers, remembering the former capitalistic times, showed their appreciation for the free care they now were receiving by sometimes bringing various food products. It was more than I needed for myself. Once I bought and sent a big jar of honey, which was very valuable, to the Rosenfeins in Lwow. They really appreciated this, as they could smear the honey on bread in place of butter, which was very scarce. I also sent a package of food to the Lewensons in Komi S.S.R. Food was no problem, but clothes were very expensive. My salary was about 400 rubles per month, which was rather low, doctors being poorly paid. As the only doctor in the entire area, I was privileged to buy some personal items without standing on line if a shipment of merchandise arrived. However, these deliveries to the store (the only general store in the village) were haphazard, and you usually could not get the size that you wanted or needed. I recall once wanting to buy a pair of shoes, and they had all sizes but mine.

Another story comes to mind which characterizes the way the Russian security police were working, having everybody on their minds and on their lists and knowing what everyone was doing, where everyone was working, and so on. One day, at about 1:15 in the afternoon, after I had finished at the dispensary, I went to buy something from the general store. Quite a few people besides me were standing around in the store when an officer of the security police in his blue uniform entered. He was not a local officer; I had never seen him, and to my knowledge he had never seen me. He approached me and asked me whether I was the doctor for the local dispensary and community. After my affirmative reply he asked me again whether it was already past my office hours. This was about all the conversation we had; apparently he wanted to let me know that he knew who I was.

There were very few Jews in this village, but Jews in general were not that scared at this time. There was no suspicion by the Russians that the Jews might be displeased with them, as on the other side were the Nazis, who were certainly worse for the Jews in every way. At that time it was a plus, an additional security benefit, to be a Jew because the Russians trusted the Jews more than the Ukrainians. They knew that the Ukrainians were all nationalists and really hated the Russians. Many of these nationalistic Ukrainians superficially became very ardent communists, trying to ingratiate themselves and work together with the Russians. However, I am pretty sure that the Russians were very suspicious and did not trust them.

One very bad fault was to be rich, no matter who you were, Ukrainian or Jew. The security police (called the NKVD, which was an abbreviation of the ministry of internal security affairs) would drive up at night to a rich farmer's house, ask him to join them, and take him away. One rich farmer of Germakowka, Vasyl Kostecki, was taken away one night, supposedly to the next district town, Czortkow, to face some kind of charges. His transgression probably was that he was rich, there being no other cause with which to charge him. Nobody every heard from him again or knew what happened to him.

Another incident occurred on May Day (May 1), a big Russian communist holiday. The village council members and the other local leaders, who were all Ukrainians (although at that time playing the communist role), held a big rally, speaking with praise of Joseph Stalin, the "wise teacher of all the nations of the world." After the speeches they had a gala party at the village council seat. There was an abundance of food, meat, beer, and vodka. Being the representative of health care, I was invited to their party, and, whether I liked it or not, I would not dare refuse. I took with me the daughter of my landlord. I had a couple of drinks, and then I had something to eat, and then I had a couple of more drinks. Not being used to drinking, I could hardly walk by the time everybody got up to dance. I managed, though, and danced a little.

During this party, sitting next to me were two Ukrainian ladies, intelligent women, whose husbands were there, too, having some functions in the new setup under the Russian regime. (All the stores and agencies had been nationalized, so many of these Ukrainian people had functions for which they were paid a salary by the government.) At about eleven or twelve at night, two Russian secret police officers walked in, just as friendly visitors. Because it was such a big holiday, I guess they went from place to place, "paying their respects" everywhere. These two ladies were quite disturbed by their visit because they both knew the tradition of the Russian secret police. A party like this might be a good occasion for the police to pick up a couple of men, such as their husbands, and take them away without anybody knowing where and without any court hearing. Luckily, the officers did not stay long and left without bothering anybody; the ladies felt very relieved.

With me in the dispensary were a Ukrainian nurse from the eastern (Russian) Ukraine and a local Ukrainian who was working as an aide and also taking care of the dispensary's cleanliness. We had no telephone, and whoever wanted me had to come by. If it was within the village, I usually would walk; if it was very far, they would come for me with horse and wagon. One spring day I had to make a late afternoon visit to a patient who lived quite far away in another village. Because it was too late to return home, I stayed overnight in the patient's house. In the morning I had a very good breakfast of fried eggs and fresh pumpernickel bread and butter, and the patient's family then took me back home by horse and wagon.

I recall another incident, in the winter, when a farmer from another village came for me with horse and sleigh. While we were riding on the nice smooth white snow, somehow I slid off the open flat sleigh and found myself on the snow. Not realizing that I had fallen off, the farmer went ahead until I yelled for him to hold his horses, literally, so that I could get back and join him.

I also had a few private patients who wanted some special attention or injections and who came to my residence. Although I had no office there, I had a couple of syringes and injectable medications. Other than these patients, people received free medical care. This was my routine until June 1941, when war broke out between Germany and Russia.

During this period, I was corresponding with Helen in Warsaw. Because we were writing on postcards we had to be careful what we said. Although we did not feel free to write about everything that was on our minds or in our hearts, we were glad that we could communicate. Despite a poor salary I did not have it too badly. There was no problem with food in this big village, which was rich in farm products, unlike in the large cities like Lwow where everything was rationed.

In June 1941, the war entered a new phase, with Germany deciding to invade Russia, starting at the westernmost part, the part of Poland occupied by the Russians. The Germans had to pass through this area in order to get to Russia proper. The Russian government was drafting men into the army, and I, together with other physicians from the area, had to come every day to a central point in Mielnica, a neighboring town, to do the physical examinations of the draftees. The draftees tried to get out of serving if possible, and we doctors tried to cooperate with them. However, in charge of this induction center was a Colonel Nikolayev, who supervised us and told us that we should not be so considerate, that the army could use anybody as a soldier. He was making a joke of it and said, "Well, even if someone cannot walk we have trucks and cars and we can take them. They can peel potatoes in the kitchens for the soldiers, so anyone is good." This lasted for a few weeks.

Soon afterward the Russian occupation authorities began retreating in the face of the Germans' forward movement. Some of the Jewish people, especially those who were single or who had grown-up children, probably would have liked to have gone with the Russians, but the Russians cared only for those civilians who were able-bodied enough for the Russian Army. The Russians wanted those of us who were physicians to join them and go to Russia, but we did not volunteer and none of us went with them. Although we were all Jews, we did not realize what we might have to face when the Germans would occupy the area and therefore we decided to remain. I personally felt that if I went any further I would never be able to reunite with my family, even though being under the Germans would not be good either. The German-led army which was moving into our area was actually a Hungarian division which was under the German command. The Hungarians stayed briefly in Germakowka for a night and a day and then moved on further without leaving anybody in charge of the village.

## Chapter Six

# The German Occupation

The government of the villages was taken over by the local Ukrainians, extreme reactionary nationalists who, under the Russians, had played the role of communists. Following the Russians' departure, the Ukrainians raised their heads, directing their rage against the defenseless Jews. As soon as they took over the village of Germakowka, they started to threaten the ten or so Jewish families living there. As the house of the Jewish family with whom I was living was on the main road, we did not feel safe and would stay overnight with another Jewish family, who was living somewhere in the back of the village, away from the public eye. In the morning we would return to our home.

A lawyer, who was the son-in-law of the local Greek Orthodox priest, became the head of the village government. I was continuing my work in the dispensary, not feeling secure but also feeling that I had no choice. I actually was anxious to leave. One day the village head came in and officially announced to me that "in the name of the Independent Ukrainian Republic we request and authorize you to continue to work in this dispensary." Of the few Jews, some ran away and some were in hiding. Being a physician and having to work in the dispensary, I could not hide. Some of the villagers were starting to threaten me verbally and quite violently, getting ready for some type of a pogrom (a riot targeted against the Jews). For a few nights I slept in the house of Fedor Chapliuk, the Ukrainian local farmer who was my aide in the dispensary. He told me, "Do not worry, you will sleep here, and, if anybody comes into my house and wants to hurt you, I will stand here with a hatchet in my hand and will not let them touch you."

Finally, it became too dangerous to stay. Chapliuk arranged my departure, hiring for me a Ukrainian farmer with a horse and wagon. In bright daylight, although it was illegal because I was supposed to be on the job, I went off in this wagon with my belongings (which amounted to a little valise) and got to the town of Mielnica, to the house of a couple named the Kaufmans.

I had become very friendly with the Kaufmans, having visited with them whenever I had an opportunity to be in Mielnica during my stay in Germakowka. The wife (who was originally from Warsaw) was a dentist, and her husband was a dental technician from a town in southeastern Poland. They welcomed me and set me up in their home. I had some money, and food was no problem for them, as they still were continuing their dental practice and the farmers still were coming to town on market day to sell their products.

Across the street from the Kaufmans was a beautiful house that was occupied by the widow of a Jewish physician who had died at the beginning of the war. The Germans forced the widow and her daughter to leave the house, which became the living quarters and seat of the German military authority. From there they issued their proclamations and made their demands of the Jewish Community Council, whose function was to take orders from the Germans and deliver what, under the threat of various penalties, was demanded of it. The Germans would get drunk at night and go around to the Jewish homes, molesting the women and men (among them the rabbi and his wife) in every possible physical way. People were terrified but had no place to which to run. By day, everything appeared to be calm. The German authorities never bothered us—we were the neighbors across the street. They even came to Dr. Kaufman when they needed dental care. Late at night we tried not to put on much light, sitting and talking nearly in the dark. We would see them through the window when they got ready, good and drunk, and went into town.

We had no choice, we kept on living like this, not knowing what tomorrow would bring. Because I had to earn a living and under the German occupation there was no more free medical care, I decided, with the advice and cooperation of the Kaufmans, to set up a little office. I put out a sign making myself available to the farmers from the various villages and to the local townspeople. Besides me there were one or two doctors in Mielnica. When the farmers would come to the Kaufmans (she being the only dentist in town), they would come to me too, and so I did pretty well. Money had no value at that time, and the farmers paid us with their products, which were abundant in that area.

Occasionally the farmers would come for me to treat a patient in a village outside the town. When they would find out that a doctor was in the village, quite a few other patients would call me. Once, I returned home with a wagon loaded with enough farm products to feed the entire Kaufman household for a few days.

In the meantime, the Germans occupied Romania. We were located near the original Romanian-Polish border, not far from Chernovietz, a big town in Romania with a fair number of Jews. The Germans chased out the Jews from Chernovietz and its vicinity, who then ran without any direction or goal, many of them coming to Mielnica. One young woman from Chernovietz found a home in the Kaufmans' house, which was quite spacious.

I should mention that on their topcoats Jews were forced to wear armbands with the Star of David and the inscription "Jude." However, those of us who were physicians were privileged to wear a different kind of armband, a white one with a red Star of David and the inscription "arzt" ("physician" in German). This allowed us some freedom of movement, even the privilege to go to the next town, Borszczow, while no other Jews were allowed to leave Mielnica. Mielnica had no train station, the closest one being Borszczow, which could be reached only by horse and wagon. A physician was able to hire a horse and wagon when he or she had to go to Borszczow, the seat of the district medical authorities. Under this pretext we could go, whenever we wanted, as far as Borszczow.

During this time my contact with my wife's family in Lwow was cut off. The news from Lwow was very bad. When the Germans arrived in Lwow the Ukrainians organized a pogrom, during which, among other Jews, a famous Rabbi Shapiro was killed while on his way to hiding in the house of the archbishop, who had offered him sanctuary. I tried unsuccessfully to contact my father-in-law's brother in Lwow, but the family was no longer living in its nice apartment. The Jews were grouped together in the Lwow ghetto, a small congested area designated for the Jews, with each family having only a room and two or three families to an apartment. I could not find out my relatives' new address, and there was no communication.

As before, I could communicate with my family in Warsaw by postcard. Now it was even simpler, as I, too, was under German occupation. By that time a Jewish ghetto had been established in Warsaw, and Jews living on streets outside the ghetto had to evacuate their apartments and move into the ghetto. The ghetto was surrounded by a newly built brick wall, with a few gates guarded by the Polish police. Except for a few with special permission on official business, Jews were not allowed to leave the ghetto.

My family asked me whether I would like to return to Warsaw to join them. Being under the Germans anyway, I certainly wanted to return. The problem was that a Jew was not allowed to travel by train. I could get by horse and wagon to Borszczow, but I was not allowed to board the train there. Through official channels—the Jewish Council of Warsaw as an intermediary with the German authorities—my family was trying to get permission for me to travel by train to Warsaw. This effort by them took many months and ended without success.

I did not know what to do. Some people were smuggling themselves to Warsaw from Lwow. My family had written to me about a woman named

Tenenbaum, who was Jewish but pretended to be non-Jewish. A nice-looking blond with a non-Jewish passport, Mrs. Tenenbaum was in the business of smuggling people. She would buy the train tickets and make some changes in the passports of the people whom she smuggled. The Jews in Mielnica retained their Russian passports, which contained each person's nationality, the Jews' being "Hebrew." I heard from my family in Warsaw that Mrs. Tenenbaum was in Lwow, from where she had smuggled home Solomon, the younger cousin who, in November 1939, had come with me to Lwow and had remained there with his uncle.

My family tried to persuade me to agree to the trip. Being usually legally minded, I did not go along with that idea, despite being very eager to join my family. One day this Mrs. Tenenbaum, somehow knowing my address, came to me in Mielnica. Without telling my family, agreeing on any price, or making any deal for putting money in escrow (as she usually would do), she just walked in unexpectedly on me at the Kaufmans. Introducing herself, she asked me whether I would like to go with her, to smuggle myself home to Warsaw. Despite having refused until then, at that moment, no longer thinking logically but emotionally, I said "yes."

*Henry at age 3, Warsaw, 1912.*

*Henry's bar mitzvah photograph, Warsaw, May 1922.*

*Henry with his parents, Samuel and Judith, Warsaw, undated photograph.*

*Henry (standing, second from right) and other inmates after liberation in Garmisch-Partenkirchen, Germany, May 5, 1945.*

*Henry, Garmisch-Partenkirchen, Germany, June 12, 1945.*

*Henry with General Dwight Eisenhower during the latter's tour of the Stuttgart, Germany, Displaced Persons camp, October 1945.*

*Henry (standing, top left) and fellow emigrants in Stuttgart train bound for Bremen, Germany, April 28, 1946.*

*Henry (bottom row, second from right) with his cousin, Nathan (bottom row, second from left), in front of Stuttgart-to-Bremen train, April 28, 1946.*

*Henry on internship at Israel Zion Hospital, Brooklyn, New York, June 7, 1947.*

*Henry and Celia's wedding photograph, New York, February 22, 1948.*

# Chapter Seven

# Return to Warsaw

As I did not have much luggage, it didn't take me long to prepare myself. I hired a horse and wagon for the next morning and the next day went with Mrs. Tenenbaum to Borszczow, where I was legally allowed to go. When we approached the railway station, she said, "Now you have to become a non-Jew, pretend to be a non-Jew." She bought the tickets for the two of us to the next town, Czortkow. Needing to get rid of my armband, I went into the men's restroom at the railway station, where I took it off, put it in the garbage can, and walked out. Of course, some persons might have noticed me before with the armband and now without it. There could be people spying (not uncommon at that time), but that was the chance that I had to take. I boarded the train to get to Czortkow. As luck would have it, I noticed through the train window that some of my "dear neighbors," the German military authorities from across the street from the Kaufmans' house in Mielnica, happened to also be going. Fortunately, they did not get into the same car where I was sitting with Mrs. Tenenbaum, but I had to watch out when getting off in Czortkow that they should not see me. I am sure that they knew my face, having seen me from across the street, and would have recognized me.

By the time we got to Czortkow it was close to evening, the days not being long, as it was March (of 1942). We had to find a place to sleep, and neither she nor I knew anybody in Czortkow. The curfew hour, after which Jews were not allowed to walk on the street, was approaching. Somehow she managed to find a Jewish family for me to stay with overnight.

The next day we traveled by train from Czortkow to Tarnopol (the district town where I had originally been sent by the Russians for my first job assignment). It was dangerous for me to move around in Tarnopol in daylight, with my face easily recognizable as Jewish, without an armband. While pretending to be non-Jewish, I still had "Hebrew" as my nationality on my passport. We had wanted to get an early train to Lwow but had missed it. Because we could not afford to hang around in Tarnopol, Mrs. Tenenbaum took her chances and even more chances with my life. We boarded a train which had only a limited number of seats for non-German civilians, being mainly a train serving German civilians and military. Following her advice, I tied a folded handkerchief around one side of my head, covering half of my face and one eye as if there was something wrong with it. We happened to get into a compartment with a few German Gestapo (Nazi secret police) officers, where the only seat left for me was next to them. I remember well their uniforms with greenish-yellow cuffs. Mrs. Tenenbaum pretended to be Polish-German and engaged them in conversation in German. I pretended to be Polish and not to understand, and they did not look at me. We arrived in Lwow after a few hours of fear and anxiety in this lions' den. Had I been recognized, I would have gotten the death penalty, at best without torture. Once in this situation, though, I had no choice—I had to face it, have courage, and appear calm.

As we had missed our original intended train from Tarnopol, we arrived in Lwow quite late. It was close to curfew, and there were few people on the street. We had to sleep overnight in Lwow. Mrs. Tenenbaum knew the address of my uncle in the Lwow ghetto. Again we took our chances, and, frightened and having no means of transportation, we walked quite fast until we got there. I walked in to everybody's surprise—my uncle, his wife Matilda, their son Alexander, and Matilda's sister.

Mrs. Tenenbaum left me there overnight and went to sleep somewhere else. She took my passport in order to have it "fixed" by substituting the word "Polack" (Pole) for the word "Hebrew." Not having seen each other since August 1940, my uncle's family and I spent the whole night talking. In the morning Mrs. Tenenbaum came for me with the poorly corrected passport, in which the change easily could be detected. We walked to the main railroad station, which was all bombed out, and took a train to Cracow, the old historic city which until 1596 had been the capital of Poland.

In Cracow we had to wait many hours to get a train to Warsaw. Mrs. Tenenbaum did not want to walk with me in the daytime and told me that she would meet me in a café near the station half an hour before the train's departure. Having no place to hide, I went into a movie house, hoping that it would be relatively safe because it was dark there. I don't think that I watched the movie or knew what I was looking at; I just sat there until the time came to leave and meet Mrs. Tenenbaum again. I was frightened because it was still bright outside, and, while walking quite a distance, I easily could be recognized as a Jew. I met Mrs. Tenenbaum at the appointed time, and we boarded a train to Warsaw. It was getting close to nightfall, and I felt relatively safe on the train. It was very dark; I don't think that there was any light in the train. We traveled all night from Cracow, arriving in Warsaw in the morning.

It was not the same Warsaw that I had left in 1939. Mrs. Tenenbaum was planning to get me by trolley car close to a gate of the ghetto. These gates were watched by Polish policemen, who would let you in or out for some money that you put in your passport, which they would check. We got on a trolley car in the heart of Polish Warsaw. In the trolley cars there were seats assigned for Germans and seats assigned for Poles (and, of course, none for Jews). We sat down as Poles in the Polish section and, when we reached our destination, got off and began walking toward one of the gates of the Warsaw ghetto wall.

While we were walking, a young Pole approached us and said to me, "Hey Jew, why don't you wear an armband?" Blackmailing the small number of Jews living on false documents outside the ghetto was quite a popular occupation among Poles. The man possibly wanted money from us, and he continued walking behind us and talking. I suggested to Mrs. Tenenbaum that we give him some money, but she felt that we could not do that because he could take the money and then report us, having proof that I was a Jew. He finally called a policeman, and I was arrested and taken to the local police precinct, being accused by this fellow of being a Jew.

I remained under provisional arrest, while nobody questioned Mrs. Tenenbaum, who was with me, as she appeared to the police to be a legitimate Pole. Showing them my passport, I claimed (as it was written there) that I was a Pole. Mrs. Tenenbaum stated that I was her friend who had come from Lwow to visit her for a few days. The police did not take her word for this, telling me that they could check whether or not I was a Jew. Unlike in the United States, in Poland there were no non-Jews who were circumcised. Although the police did not say explicitly what they meant, it was quite clear to me what was implied. I responded arrogantly, saying, "Go ahead, it's alright with me if you want to check." However, they did not do so, stating that I would stay under arrest until the precinct captain came.

In the meantime, in order to establish whether I was Jewish or not, one of the police lieutenants took a long deposition from me involving information about myself and my parents. I gave him some fictitious names. My last name itself—Gliniewiecki—was genuinely Polish, but I certainly did not give my father's true first name, Samuel. I do not remember what first name I gave as my mother's, but as her maiden name I picked the name of one of the streets in Lwow, Teatynska Street. I signed this sworn statement, and they put me alone in a room where I sat and waited. Mrs. Tenenbaum left, assuring me that she would come back later. After a number of hours she finally returned and sat with me.

Toward evening the head of the precinct came, not a police officer but a colonel in the uniform of the Polish Army. He had to decide about my life. He read my deposition, looked at my passport, and looked at me. I believe that he had a suspicion that I was a Jew but pretended that he was not sure and, after asking me some questions, was nice and generous enough to accept my explanation that I had come to visit my girlfriend. He decided to let me out, asking me only where I was planning to stay. When I told him that I would stay in a hotel, he requested that I report daily to the police during my stay in Warsaw. It certainly was magnanimous of him to let me out with the arrangement that I should report to the police every day, as he did not expect me to report if I were a Jew.

Having walked out of the precinct as a Pole again, I expected to go into the ghetto. However, Mrs. Tenenbaum felt that it was too late for that day. I did not know her reasons; perhaps she was trying to contact my family first to get money. So I signed myself into a nice hotel on Marshalkowska Street, the main street in Warsaw, paying for the night. Mrs. Tenenbaum went home, saying that she would pick me up the next morning. It was a very long night for me; I slept little, not knowing whether she would come and how I would get into this "ghetto paradise." I was even afraid to leave my room to go to the men's room—I was afraid to show my face and arouse people's suspicions that I was a Jew.

When I got up in the morning I was very restless and impatient, anticipating my "savior's" arrival. Not having shaved for a few days, I looked quite suspicious. I did not know what to do and decided to take a chance. Without waiting for Mrs. Tenenbaum, I went out in the bright daylight to a barber and had a nice shave. From a public telephone I called up my wife's cousin, Edwarda Rosenfein, who was a dentist; by then, doctors and dentists were the only Jews in the ghetto who still were permitted to have phones. Because the telephone was not in a booth and everybody could hear what I was saying, I tried to be casual, just saying, "Hello, how are you, this is Henry." She was smart enough to realize that I was in distress and said, "Oh, where are you?" I carefully gave her my address to make sure that she got it right and said, "I hope to see you, and goodbye." Having given her this message and been shaven, I did not feel so badly walking back to my hotel room and just waiting there for hours.

Mrs. Tenenbaum finally arrived about noon and went with me to the ghetto gate. Following the usual procedure she put some money in my passport to bribe the Polish policeman guarding the gate, who checked my passport and let me enter the ghetto, which I had never seen before. It was quite a miserable sight, with unusual congestion in the streets—some people fairly well-dressed, some in rags panhandling, peddlers hawking their goods (mostly food items), and now and then somebody lying in the street. At the same time you could see a big announcement about a concert or a theater performance taking place somewhere in the ghetto. With all the tragedy, with all the people being picked up and sent away to labor camps, with many sick and hungry, there were people doing business in the ghetto in a thriving black market—everybody fighting for survival. There also were Jews who cooperated with the German Gestapo for personal benefit.

When I walked up to my in-laws' apartment, Helen met me at the door. It was an unforgettable moment. For the first time in years I saw my little boy, who was about three-and-a-half years old and did not know me. I was afraid to approach Alexander too closely, not wanting to scare him. While I was sitting at the table and talking with my father-in-law, my mother-in-law, Helen, and my father (who had come to see me; my mother could not come), Alexander was being told that I was his father. It took him a while to get used to me.

"We will never separate again" were Helen's first words upon my arrival home. She described to me how miserable and pitiful it felt to be married and not to have a husband, a different feeling than being single or a widow or divorced. Helen told me why it had taken Mrs. Tenenbaum so long to pick me up. Mrs. Tenenbaum had demanded a substantial sum of money for having smuggled me, of course not telling them where I was staying in Warsaw. My family was skeptical as to whether I really was in Warsaw because I was always writing that I would not smuggle myself or travel by any illegal ways. After I had made my phone call, the negotiations moved faster because my family told her that they knew where I was and that they could get a Polish policeman who, for money, would take me into the ghetto. (There were many such dealings going on between Jews and Poles, with the Poles doing very well in these transactions.) Mrs. Tenenbaum was very surprised to hear that and softened up, so they finally came to terms. We heard later that Mrs. Tenenbaum was caught and executed in the Pawiak prison in Warsaw, as were other Jews found living with false documents on the Aryan side.

## Chapter Eight

# In the Ghetto

I found my in-laws' apartment in a different condition from when I had left it. Now there were more people squeezed together in the same area. Before I had left, Helen, Alexander, and I had been living with my in-laws in the apartment. When I came back, my father-in-law's brother (the one from Warsaw), his wife, and their three grown children were living in one room in the apartment because their previous apartment was not within the limits of the ghetto and they had had to move in with my in-laws. Another room was rented to a man who came from Lodz, which was located in an area that had been annexed into Germany and renamed Litzmannstadt. My in-laws, Helen, Alexander, and I still had two rooms for our own use. The Christian maid who had worked for my in-laws for many years had had to leave because it now was forbidden for non-Jews to work for Jews.

A Jewish Council, known as the Judenrat, with a uniformed Jewish police force and authority over the Jews, had been set up in the ghetto. The Council was responsible to the German authorities for satisfying all types of obligations and demands. It had the sad function to deliver people to the labor camps, from which most never returned.

I needed to start doing something with my medical profession. To be permitted to practice, I had to be registered in the Warsaw-Bialystok Physicians Chamber, which was located outside the ghetto. There was a branch-type office established in the ghetto for the Jewish physicians, with a Dr. Israel Milejkowski in charge. He maintained regular contact with the general chamber outside the ghetto through people who had special permission to leave the ghetto on business. Having brought home my diploma (translated into German), as well as various other papers attesting to my studies and completed exams from Lwow, I submitted them to the Warsaw-Bialystok Physicians Chamber. After all the documents were approved, I was registered to practice medicine. As a matter of fact, this was the only source from which I later got my documents when I came to the United States, because everything that I had had with me had been destroyed in concentration camps; only those documents that had been outside the ghetto, in the Physicians Chamber, were saved.

About a month after my arrival, in May 1942, I set up a small office in one large room in the apartment not occupied by our new residents. I had a few private patients but also was working in the Jewish hospital, located on Stawki Street in what previously had been a school building. (The original Jewish hospital, which was in Czyste, an area outside the ghetto on the outskirts of Warsaw, was a large complex of numerous buildings—one of the biggest in the country—with famous physicians. It had been taken over by the Germans, to be used only for Germans.)

Life was becoming more difficult and scary, with people being arrested or just taken away by the Gestapo for no known reason. It was a life full of contrasts; some people were working or involved in various legal or illicit enterprises, while at the same time you frequently saw somebody lying on the street, emaciated and nearly dead from hunger. Food was scarce and very expensive on a booming black market, much of it smuggled into the ghetto.

Outside the ghetto some Jews were living on false papers as non-Jewish Aryans. During the time of the ghetto the number of Jews in Warsaw became much larger than it had been before the war because of the influx of people from the many small towns surrounding Warsaw. The ghetto consisted of two parts, a small ghetto and a large ghetto, divided by a street which did not belong to the ghetto. Above this street a bridge was built for people to cross from one part to the other.

In July 1942, the Germans began to carry out their extermination plan. It began with a sudden announcement on the ghetto walls that all Jews would be resettled to labor camps in the east and that they were allowed to take with them whatever luggage they could carry. People became panicky, not knowing what this was all about, although they first thought that they really were going to labor camps. However, as the chairman of the Judenrat, Czerniakow, had committed suicide, they soon realized that something unusually bad was happening. Later it became known that the Gestapo had demanded from him daily deliveries of a certain number of Jews (in the thousands) to be transported out of the ghetto. Possibly he had knowledge or a premonition about the real meaning of the "resettlement." Being powerless to refuse and unwilling to cooperate, he committed suicide. All the other officers of the Judenrat were arrested and later released without explanation.

The Jewish police (with various ranks), set up to keep order in the ghetto, were helping the Germans round up people for the transports. The Germans played a game of pitting one man against another, promising the police that they would be exempt from resettlement. Jews (and their families) employed in certain German defense factories manufacturing army clothes or other army supplies also were exempt from resettlement; later on, these exceptions had no meaning. It became a race to obtain employment in these "secure" German enterprises in order to be protected. Some people were buying registration cards just attesting to their employment.

Both my father and father-in-law were unemployed. Because their apartment was within the ghetto, my parents were living in the same apartment as before the war. My mother's niece, Judith, a teenager, was staying with my parents, who accepted her like a daughter. (Her parents lived somewhere else in the ghetto, having moved to Warsaw from a small town.) At least at the beginning of the deportations, the building in which my parents lived was protected from the Gestapo. A man living in this building was involved in some "business dealings" with the Gestapo. The German officers visited his apartment frequently, and through them he did a lot of favors for individual Jews. (When I had been trying to come home from the east, my father had gone to him asking for help.) Thanks to his contacts the building was not (at least not yet) bothered by the so-called "actions" (rounding up people) or "selections" (selecting people to be sent away) for fulfilling the daily quotas for the transports.

In order to get the necessary numbers of people, the Germans would surround some streets, picking different buildings and calling over the loudspeakers for all men, women, and children to come down to the street. They then would take them to the Umschlagplatz on Stawki Street, an area where they loaded them into boxcars either directly or after keeping them overnight. The Jewish police, who helped to get all these people together, forcing them into the cars, memorized the numbers on the cars and noticed that the same cars were coming back every day. They realized that they could not have taken these people too far east and wondered what had happened to the people.

I was still working in the hospital, which was now on Leszno Street, the Stawki Street building having been evacuated to become the Umschlagplatz. We lived from day to day. Helen and Alexander came with me to the hospital every day, as did all of the other doctors' families. A few rooms were set aside for the families of the working doctors, who had the illusion that their wives and children were protected while the police were loading the other Jews on the trains. Once, on the way home from the hospital with my family (I was carrying Alexander in my arms), as we were approaching our building we saw that the street nearby was just being closed off by the Germans, who were bringing out the people from the buildings. We were frightened and changed direction, going around to another street until we reached home. We never were sure what would happen overnight or the next day, always being on the lookout.

We found out that in Siedlce, a small town near Warsaw, Jews were still living relatively freely. My family decided to give up the apartment, leaving the furniture and everything else. My in-laws smuggled themselves with Alexander out of the ghetto in order to get to Siedlce. Together with my parents, Helen and I moved to an apartment on 21 Zamenhof Street, which was still protected because most of the people who were living there were working for a German-owned factory. The owner of the factory, Mr. Schmidt, the German national who before the war had been a tenant of my father-in-law, helped us get the apartment. Also moving in with us were three of my father-in-law's brother's four children—two daughters (the older was Edwarda, the dentist) and the younger son, Solomon, who had come back from the east. My father-in-law's brother, along with his wife and older son, Jacob, went with my in-laws and Alexander to Siedlce. Before leaving, my mother-in-law gave Helen and me some valuables, sewing a diamond into my jacket to use in case of emergency. The apartment was a large one; a few couples lived in another room, and more people moved in later. We all squeezed in together because this building was considered to be relatively protected. I continued working in the hospital for a brief period but quit when it was no longer safe to go to work.

One day the sad news reached us that my in-laws, my son, and all but one of the other relatives with them had been killed while hiding in Siedlce. Jacob, the older cousin who was with them, had managed to escape and get back to us. He told us that after a brief stay in Siedlce they had had to go into hiding together with other people, because the Germans were rounding up people for transports to the camps. Alexander was crying, and, fearing that the hiding place would be discovered, some of the people objected to my in-laws staying there. My father-in-law had to get outside, with Alexander in his arms. He was the first to be shot, with the rest then being discovered and executed.

In the Warsaw ghetto the Germans and the Jewish police would catch people on the street, and whoever did not have working papers was taken away. People were afraid to go out but had to in order to buy food, which was a serious problem, with money running short. Food became very scarce and expensive, mostly being smuggled in various ways into the ghetto. The Jewish hearse drivers would smuggle food in the hearses when returning from the cemetery outside the ghetto. Because of the shortage of other meat, many used horse meat and fat. I registered myself with a Jewish leader of a group going to work outside the ghetto on the railroad. The group of about a hundred people met every morning with the Jewish leader, who had an order signed by the German authorities to let us out through the ghetto gate for work. Outside, a Polish railroad employee with a truck was waiting to take us to the railroad tracks on the outskirts of Warsaw. Everyone had to be paid off with bribes in order to get the job. The Jewish leader had to be paid, he had to pay bribes to the Poles, and the Poles probably paid the Germans. We paid whomever we had to in order to stay alive.

There was much good clothing left in the ghetto by people who had been taken away. The wide-open apartments were vandalized, with people selling to each other whatever they picked up. Like many others, I could sell these things when we went out on our job. My father had to make a living, too; he would buy clothes or dry goods from people cheaply, and I would smuggle them out wrapped under my clothes. Our Polish driver would stop on our way to work at a prearranged spot to allow one or two Poles to get on the truck. They bought everything from us at bargain prices. With the money we would buy food to smuggle back home from the Poles who came to the fence at the railroad yard. Although sometimes the Germans would let us through, many times they would examine our bags and confiscate everything or follow it up with a beating. We never knew in what shape we would get back home.

During my work on the railroad, I sent a note to the superintendent of the building managed by my father-in-law before the war. He came and spoke to me through the fence that surrounded the area. I asked him for help in getting my wife and me Aryan papers or perhaps in finding some hiding place for us. Some Jews were living outside the ghetto on fake documents (such as baptism papers) or were hiding in the countryside on farms. The first alternative was probably unrealistic because of our definitely Jewish faces. Unfortunately, he could not (or would not) do anything for us.

Edwarda, my cousin the dentist, set up a dental office in our room, with a dental chair and many shelves full of medicine bottles. The shelves were on a door to another room, making the door appear to be part of the wall. This other room later became a hiding place. As time went on, the Germans would raid apartments at night, while the occupants were sleeping; therefore, we had to have a room in which to hide. As soon as we heard some commotion we would run behind the door covered with shelves into the hidden room.

Later on, the couples from the other rooms in the apartment found out about our concealed room and joined us when a raid was feared. My parents, too old to run fast, were living in the kitchen, which was permanently closed off. To get to the kitchen you had to crawl through a hole in the wall behind the toilet. Some people were hiding in the basement. For a while the Germans were at a loss to catch people in our and other buildings. They knew that people were around because they saw them during the day, but where did they go at night?

During their searches of our building, we would hear the Germans going through the other rooms in the apartment, moving things about. They would go through the whole apartment without finding anybody. Suspecting that there were hidden rooms, they would announce over bullhorns that wherever there was somebody in a room the windows should be opened. When searching apartments, they would open the windows in every room. Other soldiers, standing in the street, could see which windows were not open, indicating a hidden room. During these searches, our window would be closed, with us lying on the floor. On one occasion I took a chance and opened the window (Warsaw windows were the casement type), reaching with my arm from the floor and trying not to be noticed by the soldiers in the street looking up (our apartment was on the second floor).

Finally the Germans saw that there were some people left in the ghetto but could not discover them. They realized that people were hiding somewhere and decided to set the buildings on fire in order to clear out the ghetto. In the meantime, a very active underground resistance was being organized in the ghetto. The resistance had some contacts with the outside (mostly with Polish socialists) through the sewers. Nobody could go through the ghetto gates, which were watched by the Germans, who knew of the resistance build-up in the ghetto. Our house was near a gate, and one morning in early April 1943, during Passover, I saw German soldiers in full gear marching into the ghetto, apparently for a final clean-up. The soldiers searched house after house and then set the houses on fire. We saw the building across the street (the one in which, in fact, I had been born) burning. When the time came for our house we all walked out from our hiding places, as we would have been burned alive if we had stayed there any longer. The Germans ordered us to walk with our hands up, as if we were prisoners of war, and marched us to the Umschlagplatz, where people were collected and then loaded into trains. We were all there—my cousins, my parents, Helen, and our neighbors. This was almost the end of the ghetto; we were among the last to leave except for the resistance fighters, who held out for a few weeks.

*Chapter Nine*

# To the Camps

We spent the night in one of the Umschlagplatz buildings, lying on the floor and guarded by Ukrainian soldiers dressed in black uniforms. They all carried sticks, and, if you did not walk fast enough, they would hit you over the head. The next day we were loaded into boxcars on a train, packed like herring. The trip was not long; we went, as we found out later, to the Treblinka concentration camp. The freight cars were guarded outside by the Ukrainians, who were shooting at the few who jumped out of the train through a small wire-covered window. The soldiers all wanted money. I paid them 500 zlotys (a lot of money at that time) to get a bottle of water, as we were dying of thirst. They handed the bottle through the small window to somebody else, and by the time I received it there was hardly a drop left for my mother.

People were dying in the car; some had swallowed cyanide which they had carried with them. By the time we got to Treblinka half the people in the cars were dead. We were sitting and walking among the dead. As soon as the train stopped, young strong men—Jews—waiting for our arrival opened the doors wide and rushed us out of the cars like cattle. They also quickly removed the dead bodies, which were immediately taken away. They chased us so fast that in a second we were all separated. I never saw my wife or my parents again. The women and older men were chased behind a fence into the camp. As we found out later, they were told to get undressed, as if they were going to take a shower. Actually, they were going to the gas chambers. No one ever came out alive from there, but some information did get out through the few Jewish workers who were successful in running away into the forest to join the Polish underground or hide somewhere.

A group of young men from our transport, including myself, were left for a while standing in front of the emptied cars. A German officer lined us up and ordered us to pass single file in front of him. He pointed at each of us with his finger to walk either toward the camp or in the opposite direction. I took off my glasses and put them in my pocket, figuring that if one wore glasses he surely would go right away into the gas chamber. (We already had some notion of the fate of people inside the camp.) I was lucky to be among those selected for work. We were so shocked by the rapid series of events that we hardly realized the horror of the situation. Metal mugs and pails with water were then put out for us. We all were thirsty and gulped it down; it was amazing that we did not get dysentery after drinking it.

They loaded us back onto the same train, which took us not far to a big transition camp in Lublin, a distribution center for different camps in that area. One of them was Majdanek, a very bad concentration camp where many people perished. In other camps, selected men worked in ammunition or other defense factories.

In the transition camp I met some other people from Warsaw, among them Dr. David Wdowinski, a psychiatrist and a well-known leader of the Revisionist Zionism movement in Poland. The next morning they put us all in rows, ten in a row, ready to march to the terrible camp, Majdanek. We were guarded by the black-uniformed Ukrainians, whom we referred to as the "Schwartze," the black ones. One of them asked for a watch; I had a good watch, an Omega, and I gave it to him, feeling that I did not need anything anymore. At the last minute a German SS (the military arm of the Nazi party) officer appeared with an order from headquarters to get 800 men for "his" labor camp in nearby Budzyn, which supplied Jewish workers for the airplane factory located there. This officer was Feix, the "fuhrer" (commander) of the Budzyn camp. Being in one of the front rows, I was among the first 800 whom he ordered to march with him to the train to Budzyn. The rest of the people marched to Majdanek.

# Chapter Ten

# In the Camps: Budzyn and Radom

Besides myself, five other physicians from Warsaw—Drs. Wdowinski, Tylbor (with his teen-age son), Feinstein, Fenigstein, and Jacubovski—arrived in Budzyn on May 2, 1943. There already were two German Jewish physicians in the camp. One was Dr. Foerster, an older physician originally from Vienna, and the other was Dr. Mosbach, a German veteran. Although Dr. Mosbach's wife was a non-Jewish German, she would not leave him and came together with him and their little daughter to this labor camp.

After our arrival an "appel" (roll call) was held. The first thing we were told was that everyone who had valuables should give them up or they would be shot. People mostly followed the order, and I too took out the diamond sewn in my jacket and threw it into the collection box.

The next day the Germans took all the doctors aside and employed us in some sort of ambulatory station (like a clinic). We did not go out to work at all in the airplane factory outside of the camp. One of the first procedures I witnessed in the ambulatory station was the amputation of a finger of an inmate. The finger had been injured by a gunshot by a Ukrainian on the way to Treblinka.

Surrounded by a fence, the camp was guarded by Ukrainians on towers located at the corners; at night the towers lit up the camp with floodlights. However, the Germans gave us doctors a one-bedroom apartment outside the camp, in a small building near the entrance gate. A Jewish girl from the camp came daily to take care of the apartment, returning to the camp at night. We slept in our apartment without a guard around the building. Drs. Mosbach and Foerster also had apartments in the same building. Every morning we would take care of the sick in the camp and stayed around the barracks most of the day in order not to be seen as idle by Feix, the camp commander, who unexpectedly would drive through the camp on his motorcycle. We got a piece of meat or a portion of butter, which we carefully divided equally among us. The other camp inmates did not get any meat or butter, except for what could be found in the soup here and there.

When the people returned to the camp from work they first had to appear at the appel to be counted. There were two roll calls daily, in the morning and after work. Then they would receive their meager meal of ersatz coffee and bread with jam in the morning and soup and bread with jam in the evening. When the people returned from work they lined up in front of the ambulatory station. Not having proper shoes (that is, wooden-soled shoes) or proper clothes, they had wounds, scratches, and abscesses. This was the time when all the doctors were busy dressing wounds, giving people medication, or doing whatever we could to help. After we were finished we went to our apartment for the night. The people stayed in their barracks, lying on their bunks and talking about their misery. At six in the morning was the appel—people were counted like diamonds; the physicians were excused from the roll calls.

One evening a group of inmates, planning to join the partisans in the woods, tried to escape by cutting the wires in the fence. They did not succeed. The guards began shooting, killing some inmates and wounding others. We doctors then were called to give medical aid to the wounded brought into the ambulatory station.

Another sad incident should be mentioned. One day a Jew was caught with a double bottom in his aluminum dish, where he had hidden some money. (Everybody had one spoon and one dish, given to us by the Germans.) The penalty was very cruel. He had to run in front of everybody during the evening roll call, and everyone had to hit him until he fell dead. The Germans then called for one of the physicians to pronounce him dead. None of us liked to go out to the appel field for this function, but Dr. Fenigstein volunteered for the task.

People were thin and emaciated, starving and always frightened of being beaten. They worked hard and subsisted on a very poor diet. A few had money with which they could buy some food from the Germans or the Poles in the factory, but the majority were skin and bones. Their skin would hang on the bones like a shirt or a suit on a hanger. Indeed, they referred to themselves as "hangers."

The Jewish leadership of the camp was responsible to Feix for the smooth functioning of everything at Budzyn. The Jewish leader inside the camp was Stockman, a handsome, tall man, wearing the uniform of a Polish Army lieutenant (without any insignia). In charge of the inmates when they went outside the camp to work was another Jewish leader who also was in the uniform which he had previously worn in the Polish Army. As ex-Polish soldiers they were familiar with army routine, which they followed in running the camp. On their way to work, the people had to sing mostly Polish military marching songs, while being guarded by the Ukrainians on both sides. Both Jewish leaders had girlfriends, pretty good food, and separate rooms in the barracks. Although yelled at by Feix when he was in a rage, they tried to be as fair to the people as possible under the circumstances but had to follow Feix's orders, which at times were cruel.

Sometime in 1944 we found out that our camp was going to be changed to a concentration camp, which was being built by our workers right outside our camp, and that we would be moved there as soon as the new barracks were completed. The construction actually took only a few weeks. The transition to the new camp was very depressing. After a brief period we were told in May 1944 that the entire camp was being liquidated and that we had a choice of two other camps where we could "prefer" to be sent. I picked the camp in Radom. According to rumors, the other camp, Plashow, near Cracow, was a bad one. Stockman, the Jewish leader inside our camp, went with the group going to Plashow.

We arrived at the Radom camp from Budzyn in the daytime and were gathered in a big hall for processing by number, everyone having a number. The Jewish inmates who were taking care of certain chores in the camp came in to see whether they would find among us a relative because people had lost contact with their families and nobody knew where others were. A young woman attracted my attention because she reminded me of a cousin of mine named Henia. She noticed that I was looking at her and approached me. I told her that she reminded me of my cousin, and she wanted to know who my cousin was. When I gave her the information, she told me that Henia's brother, my cousin Nathan Gliniewiecki, actually was in this camp and that he had been a friend of her father and her family in Lodz. She also told me that he was presently in camp, sleeping in his barracks because he was working nights. She offered to wake him up to give him the news about my arrival.

I had not seen Nathan for a number of years before the war because he had been living in Lodz, where he was working in textile manufacturing. He appeared tired and thin in his concentration camp white and blue pajama-like clothes, with a cap of the same material. (I had been wearing my own suit from home until the camp in Budzyn was switched to a concentration camp, when we had to put on these pajamas, but I was still wearing a regular cap.) As we looked at each other in our "outfits" with the numbers, we were sad but, at the same time, happy to see one another and be together. We began exchanging information about our families' tragic fate. He told me that he had been living in Lodz since he had gotten married a few years before the

war and that he too had had a son. His wife was originally from Radom, and
when the war broke out they had gone back there to her family. He subse-
quently had lost both his wife and child during the selections in Radom and
had wound up in the camp. His wife's brother, Mr. Rechtman, was also in
this camp, as was Mr. Rechtman's wife, Ginna. (Both survived the war, as
did their child, hidden by a Polish farmer.) The following Sunday (on Sundays the inmates did not go out to work) was the Jewish holiday of Shavuot.
I walked with Nathan all day in camp while we were telling each other what
had happened to ourselves and our families.

In charge of the barracks at the Radom camp, as at all the camps, were
"kapos," Jewish inmates appointed by the Jewish camp leaders. The kapos
were responsible for the order and cleanliness of their barracks in general and
for the bunks (which had two levels) in particular. The kapos made sure that
all of the residents of their barracks were accounted for at the appel. They
distributed the food portions of bread and jam and dished out the morning
ersatz coffee and the evening soup. Due to their powerful position they would
do favors for their friends for whatever reasons. Some tried to be fair to their
wards, while others were unduly harsh and abusive and were feared and
hated. They would pick people to do some chores inside the camps, which
was preferable to going to work in the defense factories. Kapos were also at
the work sites, in addition to the German supervisors.

The majority of people in this camp, including the Jewish leader, Chil
Friedman, were originally from Radom and knew one another, in contrast to
other camps where people from various places were lumped together. The
Radom camp also had women working outside the camp in the nearby munitions factory, as well as in the camp kitchen. The atmosphere in the camp
appeared to be calm, but the people worked hard in the munitions factory
and lived on inadequate amounts of food. They were going out to work in
the factory on different shifts, some working days, others working nights and
sleeping in the camp during the day.

Favoritism was very common in the Radom camp, and, as a result, as a
stranger and newcomer I was not employed there as a physician. When I got
to the camp there were two physicians who were originally from Radom, Drs.
Baum and Neufeld. Through their connections with the camp leadership they
made sure that neither I nor Dr. Tylbor, who also had come from Budzyn,
were employed as physicians. I worked briefly in the factory outside the camp
and then was assigned to work in the camp. There was always enough work
in these camps, such as digging, paving, or repairing roads. I was doing some
digging with a few other men. When the German guards would approach we
would start digging faster; we had a password, "sechs" ("six" in German),
which meant "work faster, the guard is coming."

After some time, thanks to an influential man in the Jewish community in Radom who put in a good word for me, I was assigned a clerical job as the assistant to the SS man (a Romanian German national) who was in charge of labor statistics. (All the German nationals in the countries occupied by Germany became Germans.) My SS boss's function was to report daily how many people left the camp for work and how many worked in the camp; it took about an hour to make out the report and was a good excuse for him not to be in combat on the front lines. I was the one who took care of his "workload," making out the report, with him signing it. I would take it outside the camp to the barracks where the German officers had their desks and hand it to an SS man named Hecker, who knew me by my first name, "Heinrich." The Germans let me walk out of the camp with the daily report without a guard, apparently feeling that I would not run away—where could I run?

Nathan continued to work hard on a complicated machine in the defense plant. Before my arrival he had suffered an extensive burn from hot oil that had spilled from the machine onto his leg. He had been unable to work for quite a while until the leg healed, leaving large scars.

In the meantime, the Germans were retreating on the eastern front, and the Russians were getting closer to Radom. In August 1944 our entire camp had to be evacuated. Because the camp's SS commander had difficulty getting a train for our transport, he had us walk through the town of Radom (with many Polish onlookers on the streets) and continue out of the town without any clear destination until a train would be available. Guarded on both sides of our column by German or Ukrainian guards pointing guns at us, we were exhausted, hungry, and, worst of all, thirsty as a result of walking all day. At dusk we stopped and were gathered on an open field surrounded by the armed guards. We received our portion of bread and soup and slept all night in this open field, keeping ourselves close to each other in order to stay warm (we had no covers). In the morning, like animals, we took care of our physiological needs on the field under the guards' watchful eyes.

We walked another day and toward evening reached the town of Tomaszow, where we were huddled into a large empty hall, part of a well-known prewar silk factory. Spending the night on the cold stone floor, in the morning we had the "luxury" of using toilet facilities located outside the building, although having to stand an hour in line in order to get in.

On the third day our SS chief finally got a train, a freight train with boxcars, to take us to our destination, which was unknown to us. We traveled in these boxcars sitting or lying on floors covered with straw until we arrived outside the Auschwitz concentration camp. The guards unloaded us but, luckily for us, did not march us into the camp. After a few hours they ordered the men back onto the same train, all the women having been left in Auschwitz.

We traveled another few days until arriving at a newly built concentration camp in Vaihingen, near Stuttgart, Germany, which was a branch of a large camp in Natzweiler, in Alsace (France). Throughout the trip from Radom I stayed close to my cousin Nathan, his brother-in-law Rechtman, and Nathan's friend Kirschenbaum (the father of the young woman who had reminded me of Nathan's sister on my arrival in Radom and had facilitated our reunion).

## Chapter Eleven

# Vaihingen, Dachau, and the Road to Liberation

After our arrival in Vaihingen we were assigned to our barracks and appeared at the general appel, during which assignments were made to various jobs. In every camp there were some chosen inmates who had functions inside the camp which spared them from hard labor. At the appel in Vaihingen the assignments were made by Hecker, the SS officer to whom I had been handing in the daily labor reports in the Radom camp. He was assisted in these assignments by Chil Friedman, the Jewish leader from Radom. Unlike in other camps, the German leader of Vaihingen was not an SS officer but a colonel in the Wehrmacht (the German Army). In reality, however, Hecker and a few other SS officers were in charge of the inmates.

Hecker approved all the assignments suggested by Friedman, who distributed them among his people from Radom. These included the two physicians from Radom, Drs. Baum and Neufeld, after which Hecker said that two physicians were enough. Other assignments then were made, among them the kitchen jobs, which were probably among the best assignments, as one could have a little better food. All of these, as well, were given to people from Radom. Not being originally from Radom, Dr. Tylbor and I were left out. That meant hard labor outside the camp. Then, unexpectedly, help came for me from Hecker! Remembering me from the Radom camp, he asked Friedman: "Where is this Heinrich?" Friedman had no choice in the matter and, as per Hecker's order, assigned me to a job as clerk in the kitchen.

This was a wonderful position, despite the watchful eye of the German chief of the kitchen, a big, husky SS man (originally from Yugoslavia) who was very tough and sometimes merciless. Kitchen workers usually ate their meals in the kitchen, which mean getting your soup first before it was sent out to the barracks, where it would be dished out by the kapos according to their likes and dislikes. When giving the soup portion to a favorite the kapo would stir the kettle well, but when giving it to somebody else he would dish out only the liquid portion. After eating in the kitchen I would fill my aluminum dish (which I still had with me from Budzyn) with soup for my cousin Nathan, who shared it with Rechtman, his brother-in-law. This was a very risky action, as the German SS kitchen chief was frequently around, and, had he caught me, the punishment would have been a severe whipping. Public whipping was the accepted form of punishment for offenses. The SS man would do it with all his might and force, counting up to ten or more—a horrible sight. At times, though, the SS kitchen chief at Vaihingen did appear to be human; he knew that I was a doctor and would ask me for some advice if he had a medical problem.

After some time the Germans moved some of the inmates to another concentration camp nearby. Among them was Rechtman, who became a kapo there. Despite the fact that he was trying to be fair to the inmates, they complained about him. After the war, when people were judging kapos for their behavior, Rechtman could not take it and committed suicide. Nathan remained with me in the camp at Vaihingen, as did Dr. Tylbor, whose work involved carrying stones. The work was hard and the food minimal; people were dying daily. Among us was a dental technician whose function was to remove gold teeth from the deceased.

After the Germans moved some people to the other nearby camp, our camp became mostly a hospital camp. Each hospital barracks had a doctor and a kapo. By this time I was employed as a doctor in the camp, and the typhus barracks were assigned to me. (Typhus is a louse-borne bacterial disease that can occur in conditions of poor hygiene.) For a short period the Germans brought to our camp sick people from other camps, both Jews and non-Jews. From the Natzweiler camp (in Alsace, France) came people of various nationalities, among them Norwegians who were involved in the underground resistance movement (including a Norwegian doctor, Paulsen). In charge of us three doctors (Baum, Neufeld, and me) was a German doctor, a lieutenant in the Luftwaffe (the German Air Force). He pretended to act as a doctor, as if caring for the patients' health, discussing their medical condition with us daily and even making available to us a limited amount of some simple medications. While still remembering their earlier unfriendly attitude toward me, I became more involved with Baum and Neufeld, as we shared the potatoes that we managed to get and cook in their room, although I was still living in my barracks.

Shortly afterward Nathan contracted typhus and became my patient. Under the circumstances he was glad to be in the barracks that I was taking care of, as I was able to bring him daily some of our cooked potatoes, of which the other patients were envious.

We all knew what was happening on the front lines. Through contacts with the people working outside the camp we knew that the Germans were losing the war and that the Americans were moving closer to the area where our camp was located. We were counting the days and hoping that some of us would survive.

Suddenly, one night in the beginning of April 1945 there came an order to transfer 800 of the inmates to the Dachau concentration camp, accompanied by one of the doctors. Baum and Neufeld manipulated with the German doctor to send me as the doctor with the group going to Dachau. The bad news hit me and Nathan hard, as he was in a special position to have me look after him in his illness. We hardly had a chance to say good-bye to each other and had tears in our eyes, wondering whether we ever would see each other again. Everything happened on short notice. My group was immediately loaded on the train going to Dachau, where we arrived on a cold night.

According to the rules, new arrivals in any camp were first given showers and fresh "clothes"—for "cleanliness." Being the doctor, I was "honored" with the first shower, before the water got warm. I will never forget this chilling shower, after which I donned my pajama-like outfit and was given a number, 150383. After everyone had had their showers we marched to the barracks.

The 800 of us from Vaihingen were assigned to work. I obtained some kind of medical job, for which I received an extra piece of bread. A few days later we heard that President Roosevelt had died and that the situation on the front was becoming very bad for the Germans. It was already common knowledge that the war was coming to an end. The Germans began evacuating Dachau, which was a very big camp. Groups of people were transported to different places. I was in a group loaded on a passenger train that left Dachau on the evening of April 26. We didn't know our destination, and I don't think that the Germans themselves knew.

We stopped at various train stations in Germany, sometimes staying there for just a few hours. We received some food rations; one night we slept in a bar in a town called Seefeld. At one point there were rumors that the war had ended, and the guards started to talk to us like we were human beings, but the rumor later was corrected. Finally, in the late afternoon of April 29, our group was taken off the train in another town, Schwarnitz, guarded by a rather small number of guards. As ordered, we then marched somewhere until dusk, when the guards gathered us in an area surrounded by woods and a river or creek. There was no drinkable water and no food. The guards were standing around watching us and talking to each other. We were very cold, hungry, and thirsty, believing that this was our end. We knew that their end was close, too, but they could finish us off in a few minutes. We were closed in by water on one side and woods on the other.

When it got dark and we looked around, the guards were gone. Being so used to having guards around us, we felt lost not knowing what to do without them. We started to walk around and look around for the guards, but they were indeed gone. We could hardly believe our eyes. We were hesitant to move further in our prisoner clothes for fear of being accused of escaping from a concentration camp. We decided to form columns of ten and started walking toward a road. If someone should stop us, we would tell them who we were, that we were in a concentration camp (we were all wearing those pajamas with numbers), and that the guards had let us go but we did not know where to go. It was dark; we finally came to a road and kept marching on it, not knowing where it would lead. When we saw a group of German soldiers in the distance, we stopped marching and sent a delegation to ask them for advice and directions.

A Wehrmacht officer told our delegation that the soldiers had nothing to do with concentration camps and that they did not care where we went but that we should stay away from that area, which was close to the front line. So our group of about a hundred people continued walking but in another direction. We came to Garmisch-Partenkirchen, twin towns adjoining each other, but nobody would let us in anywhere. We looked suspicious in our camp uniforms and shaven heads. Having no choice, we kept on walking toward the outskirts of the town. Noticing haystacks in the fields, we decided to take advantage of them as a temporary shelter for the night. These haystacks were surrounded by low fences and protected from above by roofs supported by posts on the corners. We walked up the mountainous fields and climbed over the fence of a large haystack. Being glad to have found a place to get some badly needed rest, we lay down on the hay. We were hungry and thirsty on this cold night of April 30. At dawn we saw single German soldiers walking by with their military equipment, giving the impression that they had left their army units. We were lying down below the fence in order not to be seen by these soldiers, who could, in the last minute, have taken out their anger on us.

In the morning we noticed a farmhouse down the road and sent two of our group to try to get some information. They were received in a friendly manner and offered a warm drink, but, most importantly, they were told that the Americans were approaching and would probably reach this place in an hour. They also were given warm drinks to take back to the rest of us at the haystack. Rejoicing when we heard the happy news, we began looking down the road, expecting to see the Americans. It did not take long for the military trucks to start rolling toward us. At first descending slowly, when we saw the American insignia on the trucks we all went down and stood alongside the road. The Americans, having previously liberated some concentration camps, recognized from our appearance that we were concentration camp inmates and kept throwing candy, cookies, and other food packages at us. We devoured all the goodies, being elated and happy to live to this moment, May 1, 1945. We suddenly became very confident and courageous and marched in the same direction as the trucks until we reached Garmisch-Partenkirchen. Garmisch-Partenkirchen was in turmoil, the Americans having just entered and taken control of the local government, which was ordered to take care of us. We received vouchers for meals in a restaurant (we had no money with which to pay), of which we quickly took advantage. We also were told that some living quarters would be set up for us shortly. Having eaten, we walked around as free men, feeling proud, as if we had conquered the town.

After a while we witnessed an unforgettable scene. On the square in front of the town hall the Americans gathered a group of German soldiers and disarmed them. They then ordered them to take off their knapsacks and throw them in a big pile on the ground. While we were looking on, they marched the Germans off and told us to open the knapsacks and take whatever we wanted. We found in them shirts, underwear, eating utensils, and, most importantly, packages or cans with food rations; every one of us took whatever he could carry.

We broke up into small groups in order to get into individual homes temporarily until permanent arrangements could be made. Feeling exultant, we walked around the main streets of the town, knocking on doors and demanding (frequently in an arrogant manner) to be let in. In many houses there were only women with children (the men being either in the army or in hiding), and they were probably afraid of us after their indoctrination by the Nazi regime. We were loud and persistent, and all of our small groups managed somehow to get into homes for the night.

With four other men, I met a relatively friendly reception in one house after we assured them that we just wanted to have our meal there (we had plenty of food in our newly acquired knapsacks) and sleep overnight. There were only a few women, who were running a laundry business, in the house, and they made available for us a room on the second floor. They allowed us to take a shower and set up a big table for our "festive" meal. It was a mixture of all the kinds of food that we had found in the German soldiers' knapsacks—sardines, preserves, canned food, cake, candy—things that we hadn't seen for years. The women made warm drinks for us, and we invited them to join us at the table.

We slept in comfort, but in the morning I had severe abdominal pains, apparently not being used to the combination of foods that we had eaten the previous evening. One of our men got a medic (no doctor was available) from the nearby American compound, who came to the house and gave me an injection of morphine, after which I fell asleep. I woke up about six hours later feeling well. Luckily, it had not been an attack of appendicitis, for which the injection would have been the wrong treatment. The American soldiers, both Jews and non-Jews, were interested in hearing about our camp experiences and tried to be helpful, mainly with food. In the ensuing days some of our men worked and ate in the kitchens in the American compound, but I was eating in German restaurants, using the vouchers which I had received from the local government.

Gradually we spread into different German homes nearby, but we kept close, usually having breakfast together in any of these homes. Some American Jewish soldiers took special interest in us. One, a Mr. Katzen from the Bronx, New York, took a picture of our small group while we still were in our concentration camp clothing. Another Jewish soldier sent a letter for me through the military post to my uncle Maurice Schulweis at the *Jewish Daily Forward* in New York. I didn't know my uncle's address but did know that he used to work for this newspaper.

# Chapter Twelve

# After Liberation:
# In Garmisch-Partenkirchen
# and Stuttgart

In the meantime a Displaced Persons (D.P.) camp was set up in Garmisch-Partenkirchen for all the newcomers in the area. There, people of various nationalities who had been in labor camps throughout Germany found temporary residence. These included Poles and Ukrainians, whose backgrounds nobody checked; all appeared to be friendly, although some of them might have been our guards in camp. Having no choice, I slept in the D.P. camp a few nights and kept there my few possessions which I had gotten from the German knapsacks. As did all the other Jews, I tried to get out of this place and move in with a Germany family.

There was a shortage of some special food items, such as coffee and chocolate, and the Germans were glad to have us as tenants because we would get these items from the Americans. We traded them for clothes, which was how I got my first suit and a pair of shoes after the war. (I still have a shoehorn with the name of a Garmisch-Partenkirchen shoe store.) On June 12, 1945, I had a photographer take a picture of me in this "new" outfit. Shortly afterward I moved in with a middle-aged German couple who had a small house in Garmisch-Partenkirchen. They mentioned vaguely that they had lost one son in the war and that another son was a POW. For a nominal rent I had a small room and was getting along well with them.

In Garmisch-Partenkirchen I met people from both the Budzyn and Radom camps, among them Dr. Foerster, with whom I had been in the Budzyn camp. He gave me a statement attesting to the fact that I had been a physician in the Budzyn camp. Most of us ex-inmates from the concentration and labor camps had no documents to prove our identity. The military government and other agencies tried to remedy this problem. A Temporary Registration certificate (dated June 28, 1945) with my fingerprints was issued to me by the military government. In addition, the United Nations Relief and Rehabilitation Administration (UNRRA) of Garmisch-Partenkirchen provided me with an identity card with my picture. I also received a certificate from the camp office in Dachau (dated August 6, 1945) stating that I had been in the Dachau concentration camp from April 9, 1945, until "the day of deliverance by the United States Army" and that, while there, I had been registered in the camp books under the number 150383. I was given another certificate to the same effect by the Political Prisoners Office in Garmisch-Partenkirchen. Those who had been Polish citizens at the outbreak of the war (September 1, 1939) organized a committee and issued identification certificates to their registrants (who included Jews, Poles, and Ukrainians) without checking anybody's background.

This Polish committee set up a medical dispensary, which was open a few hours daily for the treatment of its members. I was the only physician there besides a "practical physician" (known in Poland as a "feldscher"), who could treat minor ailments without being a licensed physician. However, I was interested in getting back to medicine in the local hospital in order to refresh my memory and gain some experience. The chief doctor in the Garmisch-Partenkirchen hospital, Dr. Reiser, was very courteous and cooperative and allowed me to come into the hospital dispensary. There I worked under his supervision a few hours a day dressing wounds and treating skin infections (despite my lacking proper proof that I was a physician). Also in the dispensary was a young physician (apparently not yet licensed to practice medicine on his own) who was an assistant to Dr. Reiser and reluctantly tolerated my presence. I joined Dr. Reiser and his assistant on his daily hospital rounds, when he would examine his patients, discussing their condition and progress. Dr. Reiser was a general practitioner and surgeon, taking care of all of his patients' medical and surgical problems, except for gynecological ones. I assisted him in setting fractures and was even present in the operating room when he was operating. I was glad to use this time in a productive way. The only other doctor whom I came across in Garmisch was a gynecologist, who would use the dispensary to take care of his patients after Dr. Reiser's clinical hours. He resented my presence and would wait impatiently for me to get out of the dispensary.

I became acquainted with a number of people who were in Garmisch-Partenkirchen after their liberation from concentration camps. I did not know for a few months what had happened to the people in the Vaihingen camp, in particular, to my cousin Nathan, whom I had left still ill with typhus. There was no communication between distant locations until people gradually began to travel by trains that ran without any reliable schedule. Through such indirect information I finally found out that Nathan was well and, together with other Vaihingen survivors, in a D.P. camp in Stuttgart in southern Germany. Anxious to be together with him, a few weeks before the Jewish High Holidays (in September 1945) I gave up my room and my "work" in Garmisch-Partenkirchen and left for Stuttgart by train. It was a happy reunion with Nathan, who was an active member of the Jewish committee running the D.P. camp there. I was assigned a room in the same apartment where he had his room.

The military government had ordered the Germans to vacate an entire block on Bismarckstrasse in Stuttgart in order to make room for the D.P. camp. The area was not enclosed in any way (as the name would imply)—it was just one street block occupied only by Jewish ex-inmates. A committee consisting of concentration camp survivors managed the camp under the friendly supervision of an UNRRA team of a few Jewish Americans (in U.S. Army uniforms with the UNRRA insignia), who provided food, clothing, and other supply needs. In the kitchen run by the committee worked a few German women, glad to take advantage of the opportunity to get better food for themselves and their children. As I mentioned earlier, although there was a shortage at that time of a number of food products, we received more than adequate amounts of these from the Americans. Coffee was an important trading commodity, with which our people bought clothes and even jewelry. In this way I obtained a gold watch and two nice leather briefcases.

There was a dispensary for medical care in the Stuttgart D.P. camp, with Dr. Baum from Radom in charge. I was assigned the position of doctor in another, smaller D.P. camp set up in Degerloch, a suburb of Stuttgart. Each day I would be picked up by a Canadian nurse, Hazel Dobson, who was with the UNRRA, and taken to Degerloch, where I would spend a few hours taking care of the patients. While the D.P. camp on Bismarckstrasse housed mainly people from the Radom camp, the Degerloch camp provided shelter to people from various camps in Germany who had come to Stuttgart.

I should mention the unforgettable, impressive High Holy Days services, the first after the war, which we had in the Stuttgart opera house. The services were arranged by the Jewish chaplains of the U.S. Army for the soldiers stationed in the area, and we were invited to participate. We traveled there by trolley cars, which we used without paying the fare, being for the moment proud, "privileged" people tolerated by the defeated Germans. The services in the filled-to-capacity opera house gave us a warm feeling of belonging again to a Jewish community and returning to Jewish life.

A few months after the establishment of the D.P. camp in Stuttgart a general meeting was held for the election of the committee members managing the camp. My cousin Nathan was active in camp affairs, and, despite (or perhaps because of) my not being involved in camp business, I was elected by acclamation to be the chairman of the general meeting; apparently I was considered to be impartial and trustworthy. I could not refuse, although I felt uncomfortable conducting the meeting in Yiddish. Even though I had spoken Yiddish with my parents and relatives (but Polish with Helen and my in-laws), I did not know the formal language needed to conduct a public meeting. However, the people refused to let me conduct it in Polish.

In October 1945 our D.P. camp was honored with a visit by General Eisenhower, the commander of the Allied Forces in Europe, accompanied by members of his headquarters staff from Frankfort, including Jewish advisers. He inspected a few buildings and the camp kitchen, asking some routine questions. No one among us, except for a young woman and myself, could speak English. Although I had studied English for three years at the Commercial Academy in Warsaw, I was not fluent in it. However, the two of us managed to answer the general's questions fairly well without having to resort to the help of an interpreter. It was a pleasant event for everyone, following around the general and his staff and feeling grateful for everything the Americans had done for us after first saving our lives. Somebody snapped a photo of the general walking with me and the young woman and later gave me a copy of it. Years later, in the early 1960s, I sent it to him (by then, ex-President Eisenhower) at his home in Gettysburg, Pennsylvania, requesting his autograph. I received it back by return mail with his signature.

While I was living in Garmisch-Partenkirchen and later during my stay in Stuttgart, I traveled a few times to Munich, in southeastern Germany, where a central organization had been set up to register survivors of various camps, thus enabling people to find relatives or friends among the registrants. I searched the lists in Munich and also in other D.P. camps in the state of Bavaria, although I hardly had any hope of finding my wife and my parents, whom I had left in Treblinka. I did not find even any distant relatives.

After some time, people had to make up their mind where they wanted to immigrate to from Germany. Whoever had relatives abroad wanted to join them, some going to Israel, others to the United States. After the initial contact with my uncle Maurice in New York through an American Jewish soldier, I was corresponding with him regularly. My friend Shilem Warhaftig wanted me to join him in Israel. However, I decided to go to the United States, where I had my uncles Maurice and Irving, my mother's brothers. Although Nathan had no relatives in the United States, he, too, decided to go there. Neither one of us was interested in spending any more time in Germany, wanting to leave that country as fast as possible. However, it did take some time for various formalities to be taken care of after we had registered our choices.

In the meantime I participated in a conference of Jewish medical doctors in Landsberg (in Bavaria) which took place from February 9 to February 11,

1946. It was a very exciting event for me, meeting many other Jewish doctors who also had been liberated after the war and were staying in the American Occupation Zone. Later, in the first half of April 1946, I participated in a two-week course of daily lectures in tropical medicine given for a group of Jewish doctors by the Tropical Diseases Institute of the University of Tubingen, which was southwest of Stuttgart. After completing the course we received certificates and had a group dinner at a nice restaurant on the Neckar River in Tubingen.

## Chapter Thirteen

# Beginning Anew in America

On April 24, 1946, the United States Consulate General in Stuttgart processed Nathan's and my emigration papers, and, following a physical examination (anybody with a serious medical problem would not be permitted to enter the United States), we were approved to emigrate and given certificates of identity (with our pictures) in lieu of passports. Four days later we left Stuttgart by train, arriving the next day in Bremen, where we stayed in the Bremen Emigrant Staging Area (a kind of transition camp) until our departure for the United States on the SS Marine Flasher on May 9, 1946. The fare of $142 was paid for me by the Joint Distribution Committee (a division of the future United Jewish Appeal), from whom I also received $5 in pocket money. (A few years afterward I paid back all the money that I had received for the fare and for later maintenance support while studying for my medical license.) My luggage consisted of a cheap valise which I had gotten in trade for chocolate and cigarettes (which everybody received in Germany with our allotments) and two briefcases which I had acquired in the same way; these were more than sufficient for my "possessions."

Nathan and I enjoyed the trip despite the SS Marine Flasher's being a converted army boat with very simple accommodations. We slept in bunks, but food was abundant, and we were lucky to be among the few who were not seasick. A day before our arrival in New York the captain of the ship threw a farewell party for us with food and songs. The ship arrived in port on the night of May 19, 1946, and we stayed on it overnight, watching from the deck the brightly lit city and the stream of cars running on a nearby highway.

The next morning U.S. Immigration Service officials boarded the boat and began checking everybody's documents before letting them off the ship. Nathan and I were among the last ones on the list and were taken care of quite late in the day. Because I had not informed my uncle Maurice about the date of my arrival, I was not aware that he was waiting for me until he was allowed to come on the ship. He had found my name on the list of passengers published in one of the New York newspapers. Passengers' relatives were not allowed on the ship, but my uncle, having some papers proving that he had been working for a newspaper, managed to get through. After the formalities were completed, he took me to his home in the Bronx.

Nathan (who was not related to my uncle) and other people not having relatives in New York went to the Hotel Marseilles, which was around 90th Street and Broadway. I felt badly parting from Nathan, with whom I had been very close during our years together in the camps, sometimes facing death together. However, I could not help it, and, after exchanging our new addresses and our intentions of meeting again as soon as possible, I went with my uncle. On the way home I remarked to him about the streets being littered with paper, which I had not expected to see in the big city of New York. His reply surprised me even more, as he said that this was providing employment to the sanitation workers. Being excited at my arrival, my uncle mistakenly took a subway train going to Brooklyn instead of one going to the Bronx, so we had to change trains at a certain station, dragging along my modest luggage.

I stayed with my uncle Maurice during my first three weeks in New York. Maurice was a recent widower, having lost his wife to cancer shortly before my arrival. His son, Harold (an only child), a rabbinical student at the Jewish Theological Seminary, was living in the school dormitory and coming home on some weekends. I met him on my first Saturday in New York, and he gave me an English-Polish/Polish-English dictionary as a gift. He and his father eagerly listened to my story of the wartime experiences and of the fate of the rest of the family in Europe. On weekdays I frequently would accompany my uncle wherever he went for his business activities. He took me downtown to an optician and got me a new pair of glasses.

My other uncle, Irving, found out about my arrival and was eager to have me visit him and his family. As the two brothers were not on speaking terms at that time, I had to make the trip to Irving (who also was living in the Bronx) by myself. Although it was a little complicated for a newcomer, I managed pretty well to get to him by bus, having to transfer en route. The next visits to Irving and his family became routine. His wife, my aunt Fannie, took me shopping and bought me a hat, nice brown trousers, and a pair of brown shoes. On May 25, 1946, she gave me a birthday party, inviting some of her relatives. Except for my Bar Mitzvah celebration, I had never had a birthday party before, it not being customary in Poland.

Shortly after my arrival I filed my first citizenship papers in the Bronx County Court. I alerted the court clerk to the difficult spelling of my last name (Gliniewiecki) and spelled it very slowly, but she still made a mistake (which was later corrected). The way my name was pronounced in English sounded so different to me that when I was first paged in the hospital during my subsequent internship, I didn't realize that they were calling me. Unlike most people, I didn't wait until receiving my citizenship papers to change my name, changing it to Glenwick by a court order effective February 9, 1948.

When I started my internship at Israel Zion Hospital (later called Maimonides Hospital) in Brooklyn, I also began living in the hospital. My internship ran from June 10, 1946, to June 10, 1947. During this time I passed an exam in the English language, a prerequisite for applying for a medical license. After completing my internship I took a three-month course given by a Dr. Rotte, who was tutoring European doctors for the medical license exam. (In Europe there hadn't been any written exams in medicine, only individual clinical exams with the respective professors of each subject.) During Dr. Rotte's course I met Dr. Berta Rubinstein and studied together with her full time in preparation for the exam. We continued studying even after taking the exam in case we had to repeat all or part of it. One day in October 1947, while studying in Berta's home, I got a pleasantly surprising phone call from my aunt Fannie, telling me that I had received a letter (I had given her address as my mailing address) informing me that I had passed the entire exam.

During my internship another intern, Dr. Izak Goldberg, introduced me to his cousin, Celia Kaplan. We used to meet on Saturdays at 6 p.m. at Radio City Music Hall in Manhattan. I would come there from the Bronx, where I was living in a furnished room after having completed my internship, and she would come from Brooklyn; she was never late. Despite our different backgrounds (she had been born and grown up in Brooklyn), during our Thanksgiving (1947) dinner for two in the Hotel St. George in Brooklyn we decided to get married. We were married on February 22, 1948, in a rabbi's study and then had a reception dinner for about twenty-five relatives at Gluckstern's, a restaurant in Manhattan.

Following our honeymoon in Washington, D.C., and Colonial Williamsburg, Virginia, we moved into our newly furnished and equipped combination residence and office at 1555 Boston Road in the Bronx. There I began my medical practice as a general practitioner in April 1948.

# Epilogue

## David Glenwick

In the ensuing years my father continued to rebuild his life in the United States. Their only child, I was born to my mother and him in September 1949. In 1955 we moved from the Bronx to Plainview, a New York City suburb on Long Island, where my father continued to work as a general practitioner. In the early 1960s, while already in his fifties, he decided to return to school to specialize in psychiatry. He then practiced as a psychiatrist in a variety of settings (including Pilgrim State Psychiatric Center, a state-operated hospital; an outpatient clinic at the Nassau County Medical Center; and private practice) until his retirement in 1979.

The following year my parents moved to South Florida. In his later years my father particularly enjoyed such contemplative activities as reading, mainly about current events and Jewish topics; playing bridge; collecting coins, primarily United States and Israeli ones; and attending services at a local synagogue. He took special pleasure in the twice yearly visits of his one grandchild, Michael, born in 1988. On March 27, 1995, at the age of eighty-five, my father died of cancer at home in N. Miami Beach.

# Afterword: A Son's Reflections on His Father's Memoirs and the Holocaust

Rereading my father's memoirs, I am struck by the truth of Thane Rosenbaum's observation in his foreword regarding their tone of emotional detachment. My father was not an unfeeling person. Indeed, he could be quite expressive of the full range of human emotions, from deep warmth and love to intense anger. Why, then, is there little overt emotional expressiveness in these memoirs? Was the Holocaust itself too painful to emotionally connect to? Did that pain threaten to break through and be reexperienced as he told his story to me? Was his primary goal to make sure that he got it down accurately? I wonder. . . .

As a child and a teenager, I was quite docile and went along with the program—did well in school, didn't cause any real trouble. I remember asking myself, "Why would I want to add to the suffering that my father had already experienced?" I also noticed this generally nonrebellious and, at times, reverse protective child-parent relationship in a number of family friends and relatives with a Holocaust lineage similar to mine. I contrast this with my own son who, while certainly loving, hasn't seemed to mind causing me occasional "grief" by his healthier self-expressiveness. Perhaps this is partly a reflection of differences between the cultures of that era—the 1950s and the early 1960s—and of today, as well as the fact that the second generation's parents tended to be older. At some level of consciousness or unconsciousness, though, our awareness of our parents' Holocaust experiences surely entered into it.

I agree with a comment made by Elie Wiesel that one should not define oneself vicariously through the experiences of others. I am ambivalent about how some of the second generation have taken on the role of survivor offspring, making it a central core of their identity through such activities as heavy involvement in second-generation groups. Yes, being the child of a survivor is part of who I am. But is it not also somewhat blasphemous to consider that my secondhand contact with the Holocaust can in any way compare to the pain and loss experienced by my father? My fellow second-generation offspring and I haven't "earned" the right to wear the mantle.

On Sundays on Long Island in the '50s and '60s, my friends often would go to Brooklyn or Queens to visit their grandparents. This, I would realize, I could not do because there were no grandparents for me to visit.

If not for Hitler, I would not have been born. Obvious, yet chillingly true. The film director Todd Solondz (in *Storytelling*) and the writer Cynthia Ozick also have given expression to this idea. I was lucky; Alexander Sholom Gliniewiecki, my half-brother, was not—due not to any fault of his own but simply to being in the wrong place at the wrong time. At times throughout my life I have thought about how old Alexander would have been in that particular year and how his life (and the lives of the other 1.5 million Alexanders) would have unfolded had he been allowed to grow up untouched by the Holocaust. I try to remember his birthday—October 18th—each year. Someone should; as Arthur Miller put it in *Death of a Salesman*, "attention must be paid."

The relatively large percentage of the second generation who have become healers of one form or another—particularly mental health professionals—often has been remarked upon. This likely hasn't been due to chance—healing others, healing ourselves, trying to create corrective emotional experiences to mend the rip in the universe (and in our personal universes) rent by the Holocaust. "Tikkun olam" ("repairing the world"), as the kabbalists say. Those of us of the second generation have been blessed with life . . . and with this blessing comes a responsibility to use the gift wisely and purposefully.

Writers—both academic and popular—in the first three to four decades following the Holocaust tended to emphasize the psychological and adjustment problems of the second generation. However, it eventually was realized that those written about were invariably clinical samples (such as second-generation members in group therapy) studied in unscientific ways (typically as case studies and by impressionistic observations). More recent investigations, involving larger, community-based sampling and standardized measures, generally have reported few, if any, differences between the second generation and their nonsecond-generation Jewish peers (that is, contemporaries whose parents had not experienced the Holocaust). So, that's comforting— we're normal, right? And yet . . . while, as a researcher, a psychologist, and a second-generation member myself, I find such results heartening, I also know that none of us of the second generation can claim to be untouched by having had a survivor parent. The specifics of this legacy may differ (in my case, the memories of a parent's nightmares, a skepticism about government pronouncements, and an affirmation of social justice and human life as values to be held dear), but each of us of the second generation inevitably has been affected, if in ways not quantifiable by personality assessment instruments.

I go to most movies about the Holocaust—both documentaries and fiction. Often by their end, I am in sorrow or tears, experiencing misery in the suffering of those on the screen. Why subject myself to this painful experience over and over? Because I am a Jew, and through viewing these films I'm doing my small part to support remembrance of the Holocaust and those who perished? Because of my personal interest or my guilt as the son of a survivor? These are tempting answers, but maybe it's more complicated than that. Perhaps there is an emotional connection with my father that is kindled anew each time that I see one of these films. "He would have appreciated this movie," I say to myself, or "I wonder what he would have thought of it." But, of course, he is not here any more, except in emotion and memory.

So, how to act appropriately and meaningfully as a member of the second generation, "remembering what one never knew" (as Susan Gubar entitled a volume on post-Holocaust poetry), at least not directly, and helping others remember? In our postmodern era, where attention spans are eyeblinkingly short, memories fleeting, and the crises de jour rule, the occurrence of genocides (Rwanda, Bosnia, Darfur . . . our contemporary concentration camp-like litany) seems, if anything, to have accelerated. Do testaments about man's inhumanity and humanity to man, such as these memoirs, make a difference? The Holocaust ended over sixty years ago. What have I learned? What have my son and others of the third generation learned? What have we all learned? One does what one can and hopes. . . .

# Appendix A

# Chronology of Major Places in the Life of Henry Glenwick from 1909 to 1948

| Date | Place |
|------|-------|
| May 1909-September 1939 | Warsaw, Poland |
| September 1939-November 1939 | Brest-Litovsk, Bialystok, and Vilna (Russian-occupied eastern/northeastern Poland) |
| November 1939-June 1941 | Lwow, Skalat, and Germakowka (Russian-occupied southeastern Poland) |
| June 1941-March 1942 | Mielnica (German-occupied southeastern Poland) |
| March 1942-April 1943 | Warsaw ghetto |
| April 1943 | Treblinka concentration camp and Lublin transition camp (German-occupied Poland) |
| May 1943-May 1944 | Budzyn labor camp (German-occupied Poland) |
| May 1944-August 1944 | Radom labor camp (German-occupied Poland) |
| August 1944-April 1945 | Auschwitz, Vaihingen, and Dachau concentration camps (German-occupied Poland and Germany) |
| May 1945-September 1945 | Garmisch-Partenkirchen (Germany) |
| September 1945-April 1946 | Stuttgart (Germany) |
| April 1946-May 1946 | Bremen (Germany) |
| May 1946-April 1948 | New York City |

# *Appendix B*

# Map of Places Visited by Henry Glenwick, 1939 to 1946

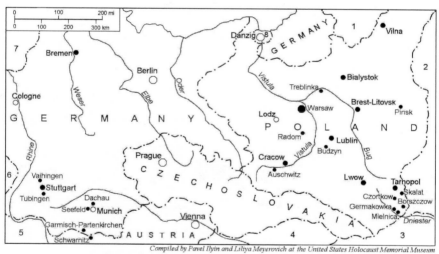

Compiled by Pavel Ilyin and Liliya Meyerovich at the United States Holocaust Memorial Museum

—·—·—·— national boundaries before the Munich Agreement (1938)

○    state capital    ○    main city    ○    other places

Places where Henry Glenwick was during the war are marked in black.

1 Lithuania 2 USSR 3 Romania 4 Hungary 5 Switzerland 6 France 7 Netherlands 8 Free City of Danzig

# Genealogy of the Gliniewiecki, Schulweis, and Rosenfein Families

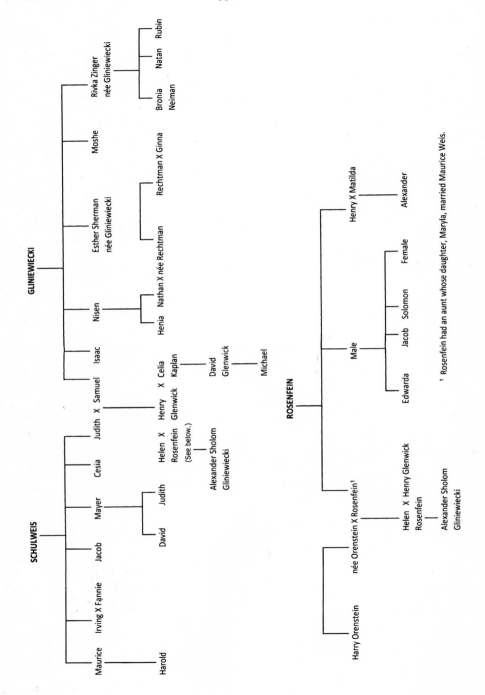

¹ Rosenfein had an aunt whose daughter, Maryla, married Maurice Weis.